The Spectacular Difference

Zelda, 1979, photo by Hayim Goldgraber

The Spectacular Difference

Selected Poems

Zelda

Translated
with an Introduction and Notes
by

Marcia Falk

HEBREW UNION COLLEGE PRESS
CINCINNATI

The Hebrew in this volume follows that of the posthumous edition of Zelda's complete poems, *Shirey Zelda* (Israel: Hakibbutz Hameuchad, 1985); the corrections that have been made to this text are indicated in the Notes to the Poems.

Grateful acknowledgment is made to the editors of the following journals and anthologies, which published some of these translations (often in somewhat different form): *The American Poetry Review, Ariel, Burning Air and a Clear Mind* (Ohio University Press), *The Burning Bush* (W. H. Allen), *The Defiant Muse* (Feminist Press), *European Judaism, Four Centuries of Jewish Women's Spirituality* (Beacon Press), *Fourteen Israeli Poets* (Andre Deutsch), *HandBook, The Jerusalem Quarterly, Lilith, The Melton Journal, Modern Poetry in Translation, New Writing in Israel* (Schocken), *The Reconstructionist, Religion and Literature, Ruminator Review, Shirim, Textures, Tikkun, Voices Within the Ark* (Avon).

Some of the poems in this book also appear in *The Book of Blessings: New Jewish Prayers for Daily Life, the Sabbath, and the New Moon Festival* by Marcia Falk (Harper, 1996; Beacon, 1999).

An excerpt from Part I of the Introduction appeared in *Lilith*; an earlier version of Part II of the Introduction was published under the title "Strange Plant: Nature and Spirituality in the Poetry of Zelda" in *Religion and Literature*.

Library of Congress Cataloging in Publication Data
Zeldah, 1914–84
    [Poems. English. Selections]
    The spectacular difference : selected poems of Zelda / translated, with an introduction and notes, by Marcia Falk.
    p. cm.
    ISBN 0-87820-221-8 (alk. paper) (cloth); ISBN 0-87820-222-6 (alk. paper) (paperback)
    1. Zeldah, 1914–84—Translations into English. I. Falk, Marcia. II. Title.
PJ5054.Z43A243 2004
892.4'16—dc22   2003062474

Printed on acid-free paper in the United States of America
Hebrew typography by Posner and Sons Ltd., Jerusalem, Israel
English typography by Nikki Thompson
Front cover and title page typography by Izzy Pludwinski, www.impwriter.com
Cover composition by Archetype Typography, Berkeley, CA
Cover painting, *Bat Galim, Haifa* © 2002 by Marcia Lee Falk, www.marciafalk.com

Distributed by Wayne State University Press
4809 Woodward Avenue, Detroit, MI 48201
Toll-free 1-800-978-7323

BOOKS BY MARCIA FALK

The Book of Blessings:
New Jewish Prayers for Daily Life,
the Sabbath, and the New Moon Festival

The Song of Songs:
Love Lyrics from the Bible
(translation from the Hebrew, with preface)

With Teeth in the Earth:
Selected Poems of Malka Heifetz Tussman
(translations from the Yiddish,
with introduction and notes)

This Year in Jerusalem
(poems)

It Is July in Virginia
(poems)

———————

For Steve
and for Abby,
once more

Death will take the spectacular difference
between fire and water
and cast it to the abyss.

Zelda, "Heavy Silence"

תוכן הענינים

I. מתוך **פנאי** (1967)

הבית הישן	26
התופרת	30
עם סבי	32
הדליקו נר	34
אני ציפור מתה	36
הקבצן הקיטע (א)	38
הקבצן הקיטע (ב)	42
השכנה הרעה	46
מול הים	54
הירח מלמד תנ"ך	56
בנחל אכזב	58
רע לי מתי אמות	60
שלומי	62
צמח זר	64
כל שושנה	66
עמדתי בירושלים	68
אז תצעק נשמתי	70
גירשתי מלבי	72
פנאי	74
משירי הילדות	76

Contents

Introduction

1   I. On Translating Zelda
12 II. Nature and Spirituality in Zelda's Poetry

I. *From* LEISURE (1967)

27 The Old House
31 The Seamstress
33 With My Grandfather
35 Light a Candle
37 I Am a Dead Bird
39 The Crippled Beggar 1
43 The Crippled Beggar 2
47 The Bad Neighbor
55 Facing the Sea
57 Moon Is Teaching Bible
59 In the Dry Riverbed
61 All This Misery— When Will I Die?
63 My Peace
65 Strange Plant
67 Each Rose
69 I Stood in Jerusalem
71 Then My Soul Cried Out
73 I Banished from My Heart
75 Leisure
77 From the Songs of Childhood

II. מתוך **הכרמל האי־נראה** (1971)

80 הכרמל האי־נראה
82 [בעיניו היו שרות]
84 בתור הילדות פרי חדש
100 השמש האירה ענף לח
102 כי האור שעשועי
106 אל תרחק
108 אתה שותק אלי
110 כאשר היית פה
112 [אני בביתי שוכבת]
114 דו־שיח פראי

III. מתוך **אל תרחק** (1974)

118 שושנה שחורה
120 כאשר בירכתי על הנרות
122 כאשר חי המלך
124 אל תשליכני מלפניך
128 החול הדק החול הנורא
132 השמענה קולכן ברכות השחר
136 ציפור אחוזת קסם
138 אשה שהגיעה לזקנה מופלגת
140 לכל איש יש שם
144 כל הלילה בכיתי
146 מקום של אש

IV. מתוך **הלא הר הלא אש** (1977)

152 [אינני אוהבת את כל העצים]
156 ערב יום הכיפורים
158 [כאשר סלעים מתפוררים]
160 [צל ההר הלבן]
164 מפיבושת
166 כלימה רחוקה
170 אורנים עתיקים

II. *From* THE INVISIBLE CARMEL (1971)

81   The Invisible Carmel
83   [In his eyes, birds of paradise]
85   New Fruit in the Season of Childhood
101 The Sun Lit a Wet Branch
103 For the Light Is My Joy
107 Be Not Far
109 You Call Out Silence to Me
111 When You Were Here
113 [I lie in my house]
115 Savage Dialogue

III. *From* BE NOT FAR (1974)

119 Black Rose
121 When I Said the Blessing over the Candles
123 When the King Was Alive
125 Cast Me Not Away
129 The Fine Sand, the Terrible Sand
133 Let Your Voice Be Heard, O Morning Blessings
137 Enchanted Bird
139 A Woman Who Has Reached a Very Old Age
141 Each of Us Has a Name
145 All Night I Wept
147 Place of Fire

IV. *From* SURELY A MOUNTAIN, SURELY FIRE (1977)

153 [I do not like all trees equally]
157 Yom Kippur Eve
159 [When boulders crumble]
161 [The shadow of the white mountain]
165 Mephiboshet
167 Distant Shame
171 Ancient Pines

[ואיקץ והנה הבית מואר] 172
[הכל השתבש] 174
[בבוקר הירהרתי] 176

v. מתוך השוני המרהיב (1981)

בחלומי 180
ידידות היסמין הלבן 182
ענף של יסמין 184
[מן האגדות שנקברו] 186
האור הדק של שלומי 188
הפרפר הכתום 190
[הגשם הראשון] 192
[שערה נחושת קלל] 194
ילדים בבית חינוך עוורים 196
מי יעמוד בפני יופיו של האור 198
אורנים נדהמי שמש 200
עץ החיים 202
[היה משהו מבהיל] 204
שיר עתיק עד מאוד 206
ראש לא מסורק 208
אי 212
ברשות הירח 214
בפרוזדור 216
הלוויתנים 218
שתיקה כבדה 220

vi. מתוך שנבדלו מכל מרחק (1984)

באותו ליל כוכבים 224
הפוגה 226
[לא ארחף בחלל] 230
כאשר געגועים 232
שני יסודות 234
על העובדות 236

173   [I awoke— the house was lit]
175   [Everything went awry]
177   [In the morning, I thought]

V. *From* THE SPECTACULAR DIFFERENCE (1981)

181   In My Dream
183   The Friendship of the White Jasmine
185   Jasmine Branch
187   [From the legends buried]
189   The Fine Light of My Peace
191   The Orange Butterfly
193   [The first rain—]
195   [Her hair, burnished copper]
197   Children in the School for the Blind
199   Who Can Resist the Beauty of the Light
201   Sun-Startled Pines
203   Tree of Life
205   [There was something startling]
207   Ancient Song
209   Uncombed Hair
213   Island
215   In the Moon's Domain
217   In the Hallway
219   The Whales
221   Heavy Silence

VI. *From* BEYOND ALL DISTANCE (1984)

225   On That Night of Stars
227   Pause
231   [I shall not float unreined]
233   When Yearnings
235   Two Elements
237   About Facts

בבית החולים 238

א. כי יימכר סוס בשוק 238

ב. מעבר לקיר ישישה חולה 240

ג. אתה טועה 242

ד. נפשי הציצה מן החרכים 244

ה. כאשר שמעה 246

239   In the Hospital
239   1. When a horse is sold in the marketplace
241   2. Beyond the wall, a sick old woman
243   3. You are mistaken
245   4. My soul peered through the lattices
247   5. When the woman

249   *Notes to the Poems*

267   *Acknowledgments*

Introduction

I
On Translating Zelda

Translation is an art of intimacy—even passion—but the story of my engagement with Zelda's poetry had a less than romantic beginning. It was early 1974; I was living in Jerusalem on a grant to complete my doctoral thesis, a new translation of the biblical Song of Songs. The Song was a book I loved and very much wanted to make mine, but my research on it had not been going well. The Yom Kippur war, which had erupted in Israel a few months earlier, had put the country into turmoil; all resources, including academic ones, were at an ebb. The national economy had been upended, and I felt the effect personally: as the Israeli lira inflated like a balloon, I watched my modest stipend waft off on its tail. By the time the almond trees were blossoming in the countryside and the strawberries were tumbling from the greengrocers' shelves, I found myself no longer able to make ends meet. And so, when I was approached by the editor of the international literary journal *Ariel* to translate the poems of an ultra-Orthodox Jewish woman known to her readers simply as Zelda (and not yet known to me at all), I did not stop to consider whether I would like these poems—and certainly not whether I would feel close enough to them to give them a new life in English. I accepted the commission and paid my rent the same day.

Up until then, I had assumed, with the poet Denise Levertov, that "I would never attempt to translate . . . poems that I could not at all imagine myself to have written."[1] I believed then—as I still do today—that to make a text one's own one has to encounter it deeply, embracing its beauties and its flaws, ultimately giving oneself over to it entirely. It seemed to me at the time that such total surrender to the words of another required a fundamental affinity for that other's voice. Yet here I found myself translating poetry that I would not—could not—have written, and that I was not even sure I fully understood. Religious lyrics infused with a visionary wildness, Zelda's poems were utterly unique, not part of any poetic school in Hebrew letters. In both sensibility and form, they were not just unlike anything I might have written but distinct from anything I had read—as the poet herself was very different from anyone I had known.

Who was Zelda? The daughter and granddaughter of prominent Hasidic rabbis from the Habad dynasty, Zelda Schneurson was an only child, born in Russia in 1914. When she was twelve, she immigrated with her family to Palestine; shortly afterwards, both her father and grandfather died. In Jerusalem, where the family had settled, Zelda attended a school for religious girls and later a teachers' college. It was during her years at the college that she began to write and publish poetry.

At the age of eighteen Zelda moved with her mother to Tel Aviv, where she took private painting lessons and befriended other young artists. When her mother remarried and relocated to Haifa in 1933, Zelda once again accompanied her. In Haifa she developed a love for the landscape of Mount Carmel, to which she paid homage in many poems.

Zelda left her mother's home for the first and only time in 1935, to pursue her dream of studying painting at the Bezalel Art Academy in Jerusalem. She worked as a housepainter to earn money, but jobs were scarce and she was unable to save enough for tuition. When her mother became ill, she returned to Haifa to care for her, never having had the chance to study art formally. She continued to paint on her own, however, and to write poetry and teach in an elementary school.

In the early 1940s, after Zelda's mother was widowed again, the two women returned to Jerusalem, this time to stay. They settled in a small, dilapidated, ground-floor apartment in the religiously mixed neighborhood of Kerem Avraham (which later became part of Geulah), where Zelda taught school until 1950. That year, at age thirty-six, she married Hayim Aryeh Mishkovsky, and the couple made their home with Zelda's mother in the Kerem Avraham flat. It was there that Zelda ministered to her mother until her death in 1965 and also cared for Hayim, who became ill shortly after their marriage.

Once married, Zelda gave up teaching and began writing more prolifically and intensely. Hayim encouraged her to publish, and in 1967 her first book of poems, *P'nai* (Leisure), was released to great acclaim. It was dedicated to her father and mother and contained many poems about them and about her childhood. Her second book, *Hakarmel ha'i-nir'eh* (The Invisible Carmel), was published shortly after Hayim died, in 1971, and was dedicated to him. It was to be followed by four more volumes, each of them a critical and popular success: *Al tirhak* (Be Not Far, 1974), *Halo har halo esh* (Surely a Mountain, Surely Fire, 1977), *Hashoni hamarhiv* (The Spectacular Difference, 1981), and *Shenivd'lu mikol merhak* (Beyond All Distance, 1984). Hayim's death was devastating to Zelda, and the later books include many poems to him, giving voice to the deep sorrow and grief that remained with her until the end of her life. Especially poignant are the lyrics in which she calls

3

out to her beloved across a chasm of silence to reach him in "the hidden world."

Five years after she was widowed, Zelda left Geulah, which had become increasingly insular, and moved to a street bordering the Orthodox neighborhood Sha'arey Hesed and the religiously mixed neighborhood Rehaviah. Situated at the boundary between two worlds, Zelda's new location was more open to the many nonreligious friends who were among her frequent guests. The change proved felicitous in another way as well: the new apartment let in more daylight, which, as the poems reveal, was a healing presence for her.

Zelda and Hayim had no children, but after Hayim's death Zelda began taking in boarders—young women, often students, whom she treated like daughters. She was extremely devoted to these companions, as they were to her, and she supported them economically and in many other ways, even providing them with wedding celebrations. During her last years, when she suffered from cancer, she was surrounded by these women and their families, and by her many other friends. Her final book, completed not long before her death in 1984, was dedicated "to the friends of my soul."

Although she lived her entire life within the strictures of ultra-Orthodoxy—dressing modestly and, once married, donning a wig—Zelda's admirers came from many corners of the heterogeneous (and predominantly secular) Israeli society. Her six books of mystical-religious verse were all bestsellers, meriting multiple reprintings and garnering numerous literary awards, including the prestigious Bialik and Brenner Prizes. Kibbutzniks, yeshiva students, academics, and soldiers—people of all ages, religious orientations, and political persuasions—were among her avid fans. As the popularity of her poetry grew, visitors flocked to her doorstep; her photograph appeared often in the newspapers; the words of her poems were set to music and sung. Naturally reserved and daunted by publicity, Zelda was an unlikely candidate for Israeli folk hero.

Nonetheless, she emerged from the circumscribed world of her fathers and mothers to become a national phenomenon.[2]

I, too, eventually became one of Zelda's admirers, though I could not have predicted that in the beginning. The first time I opened a book of her poems, I was struck at once by their emotional power and their density; I was drawn to the work but not always sure what to make of it. One of the things I noticed right away, and which became a source of fascination and puzzlement to me, was the abundance of seemingly symbolic figures that populated these poems. I am not speaking here of Zelda's frequent borrowings from classical Jewish texts—biblical, talmudic, midrashic, liturgical, kabbalistic, and Hasidic—which are accessible to readers familiar with Jewish sources (these are pointed out in the notes at the back of this book). I refer, rather, to images that seem drawn from elsewhere, elements of the natural world such as the *strange plant*, the *golden fish*, the *enchanted bird*, the *black rose*, the *orange butterfly*—simple nouns matched with plain adjectives, some of them preceded by the definite article, lending them an archetypal air. Where exactly had these figures come from? From which realms of folklore, fable, fairy tale? And what were they doing here?

I was never to find the answers to these questions because the sources I was looking for did not exist. Eventually I would come to see that Zelda's poems, like the lyrics of Dickinson and H.D., or the early poems of Blake, contain a world of personal symbols—images at once evocatively sensual and suggestive of a deep spirituality—which have great resonance within the poet's oeuvre but which are not necessarily rooted outside of it.

In the early days of translating Zelda's poems, I was hungry for information, not just about their imagery but about every aspect of their contexts and origins. And I could not help but be curious about the woman who had written them. Finally, I emboldened myself and called Zelda on the phone, asking if I might visit her. She invited me to come to her home the next day.

I showed up at her doorstep in a knee-length skirt and a sleeveless blouse, a kerchief on my head. I had debated with myself about the skirt and blouse, knowing that the very religious do not approve of women revealing bare arms or legs; but the heat was oppressive that day, and I had heard that Zelda was tolerant by nature. I didn't give a thought to the kerchief, which looked, I later realized, like the traditional *tikhl* worn by some Orthodox married women to cover their hair when in public. I had worn it only as protection from the beating sun.

When Zelda opened her door to me, a bemused smile spread across her face. "You have a secular body," she commented wryly, "but a religious head." Her poems had not prepared me for her sense of humor; only later would I come to see how much she loved a good joke and enjoyed hearing someone let out a big belly laugh. But then, little about Zelda turned out to be predictable. In that first visit, I found her to be softspoken, unassuming, and even shy, but more than anything else, she was utterly original. I had never heard anyone speak quite the way she did, and I was almost in awe of her for this, although in truth her persona was anything but awesome. She smiled frequently, and when it was time for me to leave she invited me to return. I accepted and returned not once but many times, for although I could not help but be aware of the extreme differences between her world and mine, I felt truly welcome in her home.

Over the course of a decade, during which I traveled often to Israel, living there for weeks or months at a stretch, I slowly came to know and develop a deep affection for the woman behind the poems—a woman who, despite the openness of her home, could be as mysteriously veiled and elusive as her work. When I finally dared to ask her directly about the images that had so engaged my initial curiosity, I found her not just reticent but surprised by my questions. I recall in particular a conversation that took place during one of my visits with her in 1978. The previous evening I had been to a meeting of a poetry reading group in which the members had been discussing an image in her poem "Facing the Sea" (pp. 54–55 in this book). Some people were convinced that the golden fish was a symbol of fertility, while others thought it represented prosperity and fortune. As I was in regular contact with the poet, I was delegated to ask her about it and report my findings to the group.

Zelda and I were having tea and cookies in her living room when I attempted to fulfill my obligation, asking about the meaning of the golden fish. Obviously startled by my query, she turned her eyes away from me and toward the windowsill. Pointing to a newly blossoming geranium, one of the many houseplants that filled her apartment with an ethereal green glow, she said, "See that plant in the window? It doesn't speak." She paused briefly before continuing, "Is it any less a miracle than a plant that speaks?"

Then she grew silent, and I waited for what felt like long minutes until she turned back to me. "Why," she asked, looking at me with an expression of genuine bafflement, "do people always seek what is complicated? I always intend the simple. By 'golden fish' I meant a golden fish."

Alas, much of what Zelda claims as simple can give her readers pause. Her erratic, mostly minimal use of punctuation creates a plethora of ambiguities, and not always fruitful ones; her line breaks, which tend to follow no pattern, are unreliable keys to syntax or meaning; her frequent shifts of tenses in the middle of sentences can make for dizzying narration. And this is not to mention the challenges of the words themselves—or, more precisely, of their unusual, sometimes jarring, pairings and clusterings: "the steps / of the wind's sadness," "the legends buried / beneath the ruins of my celebrations," "to sing / the heart of each flying rider, / each ardent hunter / swept to the ends of the sea."

Certain characteristics of the Hebrew language increase the difficulties. Hebrew offers no distinction between uppercase and lowercase letters, leaving punctuation to be the main orthographic indicator of sentence structure; hence, Zelda's avoidance of punctuation makes for an even greater gap. And parts of speech are fungible in Hebrew as they are not in English, allowing for multiple possibilities of meaning; for example, the words *ahuv noshev*, in the poem "Place of Fire" (pp. 146–47), can mean "breathing (literally, blowing) lover" or "beloved breather" or even "beloved, breathing"—a double adjective modifying the preceding noun. In Zelda's verse, it is often difficult to determine which of several meanings she was after—though the translator, of course, is often forced to choose only one.

There were times, while translating Zelda, that I found myself tempted to give shape to seeming chaos or make linear what felt hopelessly circular; the desire to make the poems a bit easier on the reader was a hard temptation to resist. And to some extent, I did not resist: I punctuated for meaning and capitalized where English would have done so; I used line breaks and stanza breaks to convey pauses, interruptions, and other shifts of speech; I occasionally made tenses consistent where they had not originally been so. For the most part, however, I did not insert information into the poems to explain them from within, the exceptions being cases where it was necessary to make clear to the English reader what would have been obvious to those who read Hebrew. Above all, I refrained from trying to make the translations flow more smoothly than the originals, even when the diction of the Hebrew seemed particularly awkward or unnatural, because I was convinced that the rough surface of Zelda's verse was integral to its astonishing individuality. (As we know, the first editors of Emily Dickinson's poetry attempted to "fix" it by removing words and phrases they deemed problematic; they succeeded only in diminishing its brilliance.) To my own surprise, I ended up translating Zelda more literally than I have translated other poets, including those whose poetry is far more similar to my own. In Zelda's case, I simply felt that a higher degree of literalness was demanded in order to ensure that its strangeness not be diluted.

For those who may suspect that I am exaggerating the oddness of Zelda's idiom, I offer the words of Israeli novelist and essayist Amos Oz, once Zelda's adoring second-grade pupil. In a recent memoir, Oz described Zelda's language this way:

> A strange, anarchic Hebrew, a Hebrew belonging to stories of the pious and to Hasidic tales and folk parables, a Hebrew overflowing with Yiddish, violating every rule, mixing feminine with masculine, present with past, noun with adjective—a sloppy, even muddled Hebrew. But what vitality there was in these stories! When a story was about snow, it seemed written in words of snow. And when it was about fires, the words themselves burned. And what strange, hypnotic sweetness there was in her tales about all kinds of miracles! As though the writer dipped the letters in wine: the words went spinning in the mouth.

And this, too, from Oz's pen:

> I loved the way Teacher Zelda placed word next to word. Sometimes she placed one ordinary, everyday word next to another, equally routine and common, and suddenly, in their being joined, from the mere fact of their being side by side, two completely ordinary words unaccustomed to standing next to each other—it was as though suddenly an electric current ran between them, exciting my spirit, which sought the wonders of words.[3]

Yes—if we read poetry to encounter wonder, Zelda's words give us more than we could hope for; if the experience catches us off guard, that is simply part of the adventure. These are poems that take us places, take us away; poems that go to the edge—and then some. And yet they are never put-ons, never show-offs, and, above all, never artificial: they are not "made," as so many poems are these days. They seem, rather, to have been born whole and delivered to us in a single breath. If sometimes they appear to lack poetic craft, we can see in the same moment that they also lack a kind of craftiness; they contain no guile, no trickery, no cleverness for its own sake. They are, in short, the real thing—which surely explains, at least in part, why they have had such a profound impact on their native audience, an impact that is arguably as great as that of any Hebrew poetry in the latter half of the twentieth century.

Today, nearly three decades after I began translating them, Zelda's poems remain remarkably fresh for me. Although I started the work for practical reasons, the money that originally enticed me soon ran out, to be replaced by a passion that kept me going until I had rendered the collection you now hold in your hands.

In deciding which poems to translate for this volume, I sought to make a representative selection; if I erred, it was on the side of inclusion. I had serious reservations about only one poem—by far Zelda's longest and one that had special meaning for her—the autobiographical "New Fruit in the Season of Childhood" (pp. 84–99). Although she had specifically asked me early on to translate it, I resisted for years, daunted by its frequent shifts of tenses, time frames, and locales. Yet I felt obliged to try my hand at it before concluding this project, and when I did, I found that it opened up a store of riches in its marvelous depictions of a child's inner life. In the end, I came to believe that, difficult as this poem might be for the English reader (as it had been for this Hebrew reader), it was one that ought not to be missed. At the other end of the spectrum were some very short poems that were relatively easy to translate but which I hesitated to include because I feared they might not be substantial enough. I decided, however, that their presence was necessary to provide a full picture of the poet's range.

Most of the translations in this book were begun while Zelda was alive. In the years after her death in 1984, I revised those translations multiple times and also added more poems to the collection. It is one of my lasting regrets that Zelda did not live to see the publication of an English volume of her verse, but I trust that the book is both stronger and richer for its long gestation.

II

Nature and Spirituality in Zelda's Poetry

Reading Zelda's poetry, even for the first time, one cannot help but be aware of her intensely personal connection with the natural world. Repeatedly, the persona of these lyrics—who is, for the most part, indistinguishable from the poet herself—expresses empathic joy in nature's unions, pain in its separations, as in "The Orange Butterfly":

> When the orange butterfly wends its way
> through a river of colors and scents
> toward its flower-mate, and clings
> as though this flower were the star
> of its secret self—
> an inexplicable clamor of hope
> rises in every heart.
>
> And when that beautiful flutterer
> abandons the weary petals
> and vanishes in space,
> the lonely moment wakens in the world,
> a soul vanishes in infinity.
>
> (*p. 191*)

Sometimes nature's elements act directly on the speaker, as in this untitled poem:

> The first rain—
> a plenitude of freshness
> with no sign of Cain.
> And agony will no longer
> whisper to my soul,
> "I am the king."

No longer will it say,
"I am the ruler."
Each drop is a link
between me and things,
a link
between me and the world.
And when night
conjures up the abyss,
the abyss conjures up
fields and gardens.

(p. 193)

The last four lines here describe a miraculous transformation: out of a seeming vacuum—the abyss—come new life forms. The abyss (*t'hom*) appears repeatedly in Zelda's work, where it represents a vast world of the unseen and the unknown. Sometimes it is associated explicitly with death, as in "Place of Fire" (pp. 146–47) and "Heavy Silence" (pp. 121–22); sometimes it is attached to the realm of the soul, as in "Distant Shame" (pp. 166–67) and "The Crippled Beggar 1" (pp. 38–41) (where it appears in the plural form, *hat'homot*, and is translated as "the depths"). Like the primeval "void-and-chaos" (*tohu vavohu*), to which it is linked in the biblical creation story, Zelda's abyss is at once foreboding and fecund. In the untitled poem above, as in "About Facts" (pp. 236–37), it becomes a source of awakening and regeneration.

In some poems, such as "The Old House" (pp. 26–29), Zelda links the abyss to the "Nothingness" (*ha'ayin*), a kabbalistic term signifying the ineffable qualities of God. The Nothingness, too, can give birth to new growth, as in "Enchanted Bird":

When the feeble body
is about to fall

13

and reveals its fear of death
to the soul,
the lowly tree of routine,
devoured by dust,
suddenly sprouts green leaves.
For out of the scent of Nothingness
the tree blossoms—
glorious, beautiful.
And in its crown—
an enchanted bird.

(*p. 137*)

In poems like these and many others, death and darkness exist alongside nature's constant renewals, which provide relief from agony and despair. Yet rarely in these lyrics does nature act with intentionality toward human beings, and even when it does, it seems largely indifferent to human longings. This indifference is the subject of the fable-like poem "Moon Is Teaching Bible":

Moon is teaching Bible.
Cyclamen, Poppy, and Mountain
listen with joy.
Only the girl cries.
Poppy can't hear her crying—
Poppy is blazing in Torah,
Poppy is burning like the verse.
Cyclamen doesn't listen to the crying—
Cyclamen swoons
from the sweetness of the secret.
Mountain won't hear her crying—
Mountain is sunk
in thought.

> But here comes Wind,
> soft and fragrant,
> to honor hope, to sing
> the heart of each flying rider,
> each ardent hunter
> swept to the ends of the sea.
>
> *(p. 57)*

We are vividly reminded here of the distinctions between the human soul and the soul of nature: while the natural elements swoon with joy, the girl's weeping goes unheeded. Even when, in the second stanza, the Wind arrives heroically on the scene, it is not to rescue the girl but to "honor hope" and "sing the heart" of all humanity. Cold comfort for the poem's weeper.

The contrast between human emotion and the spirit of the (rest of the) world is at times portrayed—paradoxically—in a context of intimacy, even eros, as in "Facing the Sea":

> When I set free
> the golden fish,
> the sea laughed
> and held me close
> to his open heart,
> to his streaming heart.
> Then we sang together,
> he and I:
> "My soul will not die.
> Can decay
> rule a living stream?"
> So he sang
> of his clamoring soul
> and I sang
> of my soul in pain.
>
> *(p. 55)*

As the sea embraces her, the speaker becomes aware of the distance between his joyously "clamoring soul" and her own "soul in pain." In "Strange Plant," a similar dissonance is described, as a flower celebrates by pouring its gold onto the grief of the speaker's face:

> At midnight, a candle glowed
> in the heart
> of a blood-red flower.
> At midnight, on the grief
> of my face,
> a strange plant's celebration
> streamed like gold.
>
> *(p. 65)*

This small poem is built entirely from seeming oppositions: the vaginal, blood-red flower and the streaming-gold, phallic candle; the heart (body) and the face (spirit); grief and celebration; humanity and nature, implicitly represented by the speaker and her subject matter. But the dualisms are actually collapsed in the poem's central image: the strange plant is androgynous, containing both flower and candle. Sensual and sentient, it possesses body, which provides its blood-red color, and spirit, by means of which it celebrates. In the poem's second half, nature's androgynous body-spirit becomes one with the human speaker, as celebration melds with grief and seeming polarities fall away. Against the background of the speaker's isolation, the poem describes a moment of passionate union.

Such union of the self with the natural world provides the climax to many of Zelda's poems; often, however, the epiphany is followed by withdrawal into separateness. When, for example, in "Sun-Startled Pines," the poet's sense of smell reconnects her with the pine trees and ultimately with the world, another part of the self intercedes—in midsentence, as it were—to question, and thus halt, the experience. In an instant, the speaker is returned from ecstasy to isolation, as the world becomes once more a bewildering place in which meaning will not be found:

> Sun-startled pines
> wafted a wild fragrance—
> the same stunning strength
> from the inmost flowering
> made the world my home again
> but did not reveal the core,
> the divine intention
> in budding and wilting plants.
> And the point of my life
> and the point of my death—
> I will not know in this world.
>
> *(p. 201)*

The disappointment and doubt that enter in the sixth line are part of a cognitive process in which sensory, nonrational perception is followed by attempts to analyze and explain. But because the doubt is articulated so soon after the union is described, one may wonder whether it does not also reflect some underlying conflict within the poet's self.

At times Zelda articulates this conflict explicitly, as in "Distant Shame":

> 1 I am bound in gratitude
> to a pale green leaf—
> for a leaf
> is a hand
> that pulls my soul from the abyss
> with a simple, silky affection,

7 with no judgment about my life;
   for a leaf is a startling story of freshness
   and revival of the dead.
   But my lot remains with people—
   and in the presence of people
   with their inclination to betray,
   I open up the storehouse of my mind
   and expose my pain.

15 To the sadness of wilting plants
   and to the sorrow of the beasts
   only my senses respond.
   My soul stands on another planet
   and responds to human terror
   and distant shame.
   . . . .

(p. 167)

In lines 1–7, the poet describes how she is drawn from the abyss by the nonjudgmental affection of a leaf. In lines 15–20, however, she insists that only her senses—not her entire self—responds to the natural world.

The tension in this poem might be understood this way: Part of the persona, the "senses," intuits a strong connection between self and other, an empathic bond capable of transcending the barriers between the species of life. This aspect of the self leads the speaker directly into moments of oneness with the universe. Yet the theology of traditional Judaism is steeped in the value of separation—between God and world, between the sacred and the profane, between male and female, certainly between the distinct species of the natural world. It is true, of course, that Hasidic Judaism, the tradition in which Zelda was raised, contains mystical teachings that celebrate nature and also emphasize intimacy with the divine. Still, in the basic theology of the rabbis upon which even Hasidism rests, the maintenance of boundaries is crucial. According to the biblical story, it is humanity, as distinct from the rest of creation, that is made "in God's image," human beings—and not the other life forms—with whom God communicates directly.

This traditional belief-system is given voice in Zelda's poems through the part of her persona that she often refers to as her "soul"; it is the soul that pulls back from the unitive experiences of the senses. It is as though the poet wants to preserve the traditional theological order, even—or especially—in the presence of countervailing sensations and perceptions. In an untitled poem, Zelda points to the theological nature of this conflict:

1 I do not like all trees equally—
my soul befriends a pear tree
that is sick.

. . . .

15 In this yard, I stand
before a tree whose end is near—
the crown of its freshness has fallen,
and its once sweet, once fragrant fruits,
which delighted and freed the soul,
are like brown caves,
swarming with tiny snakes.

22 But all this sorrow
belongs to quiet nights.
On the day of God's wrath,
I don't beg mercy for it,
I do not beg for it,
for my soul is removed from the plants.

28 And yet, how I suffered
   when a small peach tree
   that I raised in a bucket
   was trampled
   on the eve of Judgment Day.

   (p. 153)

The speaker's ambivalence here is profound; the movement
of the poem turns not once but twice, as she first expresses
(lines 1–3 of the translation), then denies (lines 22–27), then
reclaims (lines 28–32) her empathy with the trees. This to-
and-fro movement reveals a struggle between the truths of
the senses and conscious theological belief. To the God from
whom the speaker might "beg mercy," the tree is not a proper
cause for petition. Yet she cannot escape the awareness of her
pain, which she feels to be in response to the suffering of the
trees.

While God is only referred to in this poem, elsewhere
he is explicitly addressed (as in essentially all the traditional
Hebrew liturgy, the God of these poems is a male sovereign;
the gender, which may not always be apparent in the English
translation, is clear in the original Hebrew). He is consistently
a supernatural being who is separate from—"other than"—his
creation. It is to this being that the poet turns for help in her
weakness, her dependency, her despair. Yet her rescue often
comes from the world itself as it enters her daily life—from a
tree or a flower or a garden, from the wind or the sun or the
sea, sometimes from another human being. In a small untitled
poem, she describes one of these transforming moments:
In the morning, I thought:

> "Life's magic will never return,
> it won't return."
> Suddenly in my house, the sun

is a living thing,
and the table with its bread—
gold.
And the flower and the cups—
gold.
And the sadness?
Even there—
radiance.

(p. 177)

These encounters with the everyday world are what repeatedly offer joy and hope, drawing the self out of isolation and into a state of belonging. And it is always the senses—sight and smell and taste, touch and hearing—that bring in light and fragrance and fruit, silky affection and song. That is, the speaker of these poems attains spiritual wholeness by means of her sensuality; and athough she explicitly ascribes power to the Creator, she is empowered by her contacts with the creation.

Thus, while utilizing the dualistic categories characteristic of traditional rabbinic theology—soul/body, God/nature—Zelda's poetry ultimately transforms their meaning. By revealing the power of what has traditionally been seen as weak or small, the poet modulates, if not quite subverts, the hierarchy she otherwise accepts. A devout Jew and a believer in an omnipotent God, she seems to intuit truths that are not fully expressible in the terms of the theological system she has inherited. She does not reject that system; she does not philosophize at all. She only recounts her stories, speaking in the most personal way of her memories, her longings, her dreams, her fears. When she does so, divisions and distinctions tend to fall away—as in the poem from which the title of this English collection is taken, "Heavy Silence":

Death will take the spectacular difference
between fire and water
and cast it to the abyss.

Heavy silence
will crouch like a bull
on the names that humans have given
to the birds of the sky
and the beasts of the field,
the evening skies,
the vast distances in space,
and things hidden from the eye.

Heavy silence will crouch like a bull
on all the words.
And it will be as hard for me to part
from the names of things
as from the things themselves.

O Knower of Mysteries,
help me understand
what to ask for
on the final day.

(p. 221)

Facing life's ultimate reality, the poet knows that words—
the only means we have with which to make distinctions—are,
finally, useless. Zelda petitions here and throughout her work
for help in confronting the inevitable heaviness—the sorrow,
the grief, the despair—and the silence, which takes the forms
of the pit, the abyss, the depths, the Nothingness, and the hid-
den world. Repeatedly, she pleads for guidance to see beyond
the pain and darkness that threaten to overtake her. And yet
she is not entirely without her own resources: she is guided

throughout by a penetrating vision that reveals itself in the radiant cosmos of her imagery. In this world of her own creation, myriad aspects of nature emerge as sources of transforming power.

For the poet, it will always be hard "to part from the names of things." Yet the author of these poems knows well how traditional naming can fail her, leaving essential questions unanswered, the quest for meaning unfulfilled. In the face of this knowledge, she forges a personal idiom that might aptly be described—in her own words—as one of spectacular difference.

---

[1] Eugene Guillevic, *Selected Poems*, trans. Denise Levertov (New York: New Directions, 1969), xiii.

[2] The biographical information about Zelda included in this Introduction comes from personal acquaintance with the poet, supplemented by Hamutal Bar-Yosef's monograph *Al shirat Zelda* (On the Poetry of Zelda) (Israel: Hakibbutz Hameuchad, 1988). Bar-Yosef includes a bibliography of other Hebrew works on Zelda.

[3] Amos Oz, *Sipur al ahavah v'hoshekh* (A Tale of Love and Darkness) (Jerusalem: Keter, 2002), 337, 334.

Note:
When a poem continues beyond a page, it does so without a stanza break.

I

ﬡﬡﬡ
Leisure

1967

הבית הישן

הַבַּיִת הַצָּנוּעַ שֻׁתָּף
לְהִלּוּלוֹת הַשָּׁמַיִם;
הַשֶּׁמֶשׁ מַשְׁלִיךְ אֶל תּוֹכוֹ
אֶת זְהָבוֹ הַבּוֹעֵר,
וְהַלַּיְלָה
מֵצִיף אוֹתוֹ בַּאֲפֵלַת כּוֹכָבִים.

שָׁם, מֵעֵבֶר לַבַּיִת,
בָּאֹפֶק,
חַיִּים אֶת חַיֵּיהֶם הָאִלְּמִים
הֶהָרִים הַנִּשָּׁפִים, הָעוֹטִים
אֶת סוֹדָם בִּצְעִיף אָפֹר,
וּמִתַּחַת לְרִצְפַּת הַבַּיִת
חַי אֶת חַיָּיו הַטְּמִירִים,
אֶת חַיָּיו הַמְיֻחָדִים,
הֶעָפָר,
וְכָל מַה שֶׁטָּמוּן בְּתוֹכוֹ –
זְרָעִים, שָׁרָשִׁים, מַעְיָנוֹת...

וְאֵין הַבַּיִת הֶעָנִי
שָׁר שִׁירִים עַל קִרְבַת הַתְּהוֹם,
עַל שִׁלְטוֹן הָאַיִן,
וְאֵין הַבַּיִת הַשּׁוֹתֵק מִתְנוֹדֵד,
וְאֵין הַבַּיִת הַמִּשְׁנֶה –

The Old House

The modest house is partner
to the celebrations of the sky.
The sun thrusts its burning gold into it,
and night floods it
with a darkness of stars.

Beyond the house, there
on the horizon,
the steep mountains live
their silent lives,
wrapping their secret in a gray shawl.
And beneath the floor of the house
the earth lives its hidden life,
its unique life,
along with all that is concealed within—
seeds, roots, springs—

And the humble house
sings no songs
about the nearness of the abyss,
about the reign of Nothingness;
and the silent house
does not sway;
and the strange house

[handwritten margin notes: "gate to the universe"; "House in the mth."; "Built upon the earth"; "She takes in the world w/o being activated by God"; "It's more abstract"; "→ w/ emotion"]

שִׁכּוֹר.
אֲרֶשֶׁת שֶׁל סְתָמִיּוּת שְׁפוּכָה
עַל פְּנֵי אֲבָנָיו הַכֵּהוֹת –
וַהֲרֵי זֶה כִּמְעַט בִּטָּחוֹן.

is not drunk.
A vague expression spills
over its dark stones—
and this is almost security.

התופרת

בַּיּוֹם בֵּיתָהּ הַקָּטָן כֹּה שׁוֹמֵם,
בְּלֹא יָדִיד, בְּלֹא חָתָן,
בַּלַּיְלָה יִשְׁלֹט בָּהּ אָדוֹן
נַעֲלֶה, נֶאֱמָן

כְּשֶׁתֶּחֱלֶה – יְחַבְּקֶנָּה,
כְּשֶׁתִּגְוַע – יְנַשְּׁקֶנָּה,
כְּשֶׁתָּמוּת –
יְאַמְּצֶנָּה אֶל לִבּוֹ הַקַּר,
בְּיָדַיִם שֶׁל עָפָר.

The Seamstress

By day, her small house is so empty—
without a friend, without a groom.
At night, a lord rules her—
faithful, supreme.

When she grows ill, he embraces her;
when she is dying, he kisses her;
when she is dead,
he will hold her
to his heart of frost
with his hands of dust.

עם סבי

כְּאַבְרָהָם אָבִינוּ
שֶׁבַּלַּיְלָה סָפַר מַזָּלוֹת,
שֶׁקָּרָא אֶל בּוֹרְאוֹ
מִתּוֹךְ הַכִּבְשָׁן,
שֶׁאֶת בְּנוֹ עָקַד –
הָיָה סָבִי.
אוֹתָהּ אֱמוּנָה שְׁלֵמָה
בְּתוֹךְ הַשַּׁלְהֶבֶת,
וְאוֹתוֹ מַבָּט טָלוּל
וְזָקָן רַד־גַּלִּים.
בַּחוּץ יָרַד הַשֶּׁלֶג,
בַּחוּץ שָׁאֲגוּ:
אֵין דִּין וְאֵין דַּיָּן.
וּבְחֶדְרוֹ הַסָּדוּק, הַמְנֻפָּץ
שָׁרוּ כְרוּבִים
עַל יְרוּשָׁלַיִם שֶׁל מַעְלָה.

With My Grandfather

Like our father Abraham
who counted stars at night,
who called out to his Creator
from the furnace,
who bound his son
on the altar—
so was my grandfather.
The same perfect faith
in the midst of the flames,
the same dewy gaze
and soft-curling beard.
Outside, it snowed;
outside, they roared:
*"There is no justice,
no judge."*
And in the shambles of his room,
cherubs sang
of the Heavenly Jerusalem.

הַדְלִיקוּ נֵר

הַדְלִיקוּ נֵר
שְׁתוּ יַיִן.
הַשַּׁבָּת קָטְפָה בַּלָּאט
אֶת הַשֶּׁמֶשׁ הַשּׁוֹקַעַת.
הַשַּׁבָּת יוֹרֶדֶת לְאַט
וּבְיָדָהּ שׁוֹשַׁנַּת הָרְקִיעִים.

אֵיךְ תִּשְׁתֹּל הַשַּׁבָּת
פֶּרַח עָצוּם וּמֵאִיר
בְּלֵב צַר וְעִוֵּר?
אֵיךְ תִּשְׁתֹּל הַשַּׁבָּת
אֶת צִיץ הַמַּלְאָכִים
בְּלֵב בָּשָׂר מְשֻׁגָּע וְהוֹלֵל?
הֲתִצְמַח שׁוֹשַׁנַּת הָאַלְמָוֶת
בְּדוֹר שֶׁל עֲבָדִים
לַהֶרֶס,
בְּדוֹר שֶׁל עֲבָדִים
לַמָּוֶת?!

הַדְלִיקוּ נֵר!
שְׁתוּ יַיִן!
הַשַּׁבָּת יוֹרֶדֶת בַּלָּאט
וּבְיָדָהּ הַפֶּרַח,
וּבְיָדָהּ
הַשֶּׁמֶשׁ הַשּׁוֹקַעַת...

Light a Candle

Light a candle,
drink wine.
Softly the Sabbath has plucked
the sinking sun.
Slowly the Sabbath descends,
the rose of heaven in her hand.

How can the Sabbath
plant a huge and shining flower
in a blind and narrow heart?
How can the Sabbath
plant the bud of angels
in a heart of raving flesh?
Can the rose of immortality grow
in a generation enslaved
to destruction,
a generation enslaved
to death?

Light a candle!
Drink wine!
Slowly the Sabbath descends
and in her hand the flower,
and in her hand
the sinking sun.

אני ציפור מתה

אֲנִי צִפּוֹר מֵתָה,
צִפּוֹר אַחַת שֶׁמֵּתָה.
צִפּוֹר עוֹטָה מְעִיל אָפֹר
בְּלֶכְתִּי, לֵץ מַפְטִיר לְעֻמָּתִי.

פֶּתַע אֲפָפַתְנִי שְׁתִיקָתְךָ –
חַי עוֹלָמִים.
בְּשׁוּק שׁוֹקֵק עוֹף מֵת יָשִׁיר –
רַק אַתָּה קַיָּם.
בְּשׁוּק שׁוֹקֵק מְדַדָּה צִפּוֹר עִם שִׁיר
נִסְתָּר.

I Am a Dead Bird

I am a dead bird,
one bird that has died.
A bird cloaked in a gray coat.
A scoffer mocks me as I walk.

Suddenly Your silence envelops me,
O Ever-living One.
In a teeming market, a dead fowl sings:
"Only You exist."
In a teeming market, a bird hobbles
with a hidden song.

הקבצן הקיטע (א)

הַקַבְּצָן הַקִּטֵעַ בּוֹכֶה,
בִּכְיוֹ מְכַסֶּה אֶת עֵין הַשֶּׁמֶשׁ,
מַסְתִּיר אֶת הַפְּרָחִים.
בִּכְיוֹ –
חַיִץ עָשֵׁן בֵּינִי וּבֵין אֱלֹהִים.
הַקַבְּצָן הַקִּטֵעַ תּוֹבֵעַ
שֶׁאָטִיל כָּל חַיַּי
אֶל כַּפּוֹ –
אֶת הַנִּגְלוֹת וְאֶת הַנִּסְתָּרוֹת,
אֶת כָּל שֶׁעָלוּל הָיָה לָבוֹא
אֶת כָּל שֶׁעָתִיד לִהְיוֹת.

הַקַבְּצָן הַקִּטֵעַ תּוֹבֵעַ
שֶׁאֶתֵּן לוֹ לֶאֱכֹל
מִן הַכַּרְמֶל שֶׁבְּנַפְשִׁי וּמִן הַיָּם,
מִזְרִיחוֹת הַחַמָּה –
וּמִן הַתְּהוֹמוֹת שֶׁבִּי.
הַקַבְּצָן הַקִּטֵעַ יוֹרֵק בְּפָנַי –
עַל שֶׁלֹּא שָׁכַחְתִּי אֶת עַצְמִי,
עַל שֶׁלֹּא מַתִּי.

The Crippled Beggar 1

The crippled beggar cries.
His weeping masks the sun's eye,
hides the flowers.
His weeping—
a smoldering barrier
between me and God.

The crippled beggar demands
that I thrust my whole life
into his hand—
that which is revealed
and that which is hidden,
all that could have happened
and all that yet will happen.

The crippled beggar demands
that I let him eat
from the Carmel in my soul
and from the sea,
from the risings of the sun
and from the depths within me.

The crippled beggar spits in my face
because I have not forgotten myself,
because I have not died.

בּוּזוֹ צוֹדֵק.
לַנְּקֻדָּה הַפְּנִימִית, הַשְּׁקֵטָה,
שֶׁקַּיֶּמֶת גַּם בְּלֵב הָאוֹבֵד,
לִצִּיר הָאַלְמֶוֶת שֶׁקַּיָּם גַּם בְּלֵב הַמְטֹרָף,
לֹא הוֹשַׁטְתִּי אֶת כֵּלִי.
שָׁכַחְתִּי כִּמְעַט שֶׁגַּם הוּא, הֶעָנִי,
בֶּן־מִשְׁפָּחָה לַשֶּׁמֶשׁ,
שֶׁגַּם נַפְשׁוֹ תֵּהָפֵךְ לְשׁוֹשַׁנָּה
בַּדִּמְדּוּמִים.

His scorn is right.
To the quiet, inner core
that exists even in the heart of the lost,
to the axis of immortality
that exists even in the heart of the insane,
I have not given over
my whole self.
I have almost forgotten
that he, too, the impoverished one,
is a child of the sun,
that his soul, too,
will turn into a rose at twilight.

הקבצן הקיטע (ב)

הַקַּבְּצָן הַקִּטֵּעַ
(שֶׁשּׁוֹכֵב בַּצַּד הַמְטֹרָף שֶׁל הַדְּבָרִים)
לֹא יוֹסִיף לְהַשְׁעֵן
עַל הַשֶּׁמֶשׁ,
קָנֶה רָצוּץ, הַזְּרִיחוֹת.
לֹא יוֹסִיף לְהַשְׁעֵן עַל
יָפְיוֹ שֶׁל עָלֶה,
קָנֶה רָצוּץ, הָאָבִיב.
לֹא יוֹסִיף לְהַשְׁעֵן עַל
הַמַּיִם,
קָנֶה רָצוּץ, הַנָּהָר.
לֹא יוֹסִיף לְהַשְׁעֵן
עַל סְנוּנִית עָפָה,
קָנֶה רָצוּץ, הֶחָלָל.
לֹא יוֹסִיף לְהַשְׁעֵן
עַל אָדָם,
קָנֶה רָצוּץ, הַדִּבּוּר.
בַּחשֶׁךְ, בָּרָקָב, וּבַמָּוֶת,
אֱלֹהִים מְנוּחָתוֹ.
הוּא לְבַדּוֹ
מַחֲזִיק אֶת יָדוֹ.
הַשֶּׁמֶשׁ לֹא תָפֵר
אֶת נֶדֶר הַהַרְמוֹנְיָה

The Crippled Beggar 2

The crippled beggar
(who lies down
on the crazy side of things)
will no longer lean on the sun—
the sunrises are a broken reed.
Will no longer lean
on the beauty of a leaf—
spring is a broken reed.
Will no longer lean
on water—
the river is a broken reed.
Will no longer lean
on a swallow in flight—
space is a broken reed.
Will no longer lean
on human beings—
speech is but a broken reed.

In darkness, decay, and death—
God is his rest.
He alone
holds his hand.
The sun will not break
the vow of harmony

לְנַשֵּׁק אֶת לִבּוֹ
הַמְיַלֵּל.
הַנָּהָר לֹא יֵצֵא
מֵעִגּוּל הַמּוּסִיקָה,
לְהוֹשִׁיט יָד
לַמְנַדֶּה.

to kiss his howling heart.
The river will not leave
the circle of music
to extend a hand to the outcast one.

השכנה הרעה

סָבִי הִתְפַּלֵּל:
"וְלֹא לִידֵי נִסָּיוֹן וְלֹא לִידֵי בִזָּיוֹן"
אַךְ הַמֵּתִים עַל קִדּוּשׁ הַשֵּׁם
שָׁרוּ בַּיָּם:
כֶּתֶר דָּמִים הַנִּסָּיוֹן, כֶּתֶר מַלְכוּת.
הִקְשַׁבְתִּי לְשִׁירָתָם בִּכְמִיהָה
אֵימָה, בְּיַלְדוּת לֹא-נִכְתֶּמֶת,
הוֹדֶפֶת מֵעָלַי בִּפְרָאוּת
אֶת הַתְּפִלּוֹת הַזְּהִירוֹת, הַמַּבִּיעוֹת
שֶׁנָּסוּ בָּרַעַד מִן הַבְּרָקִים וְהַסּוּפוֹת.

וְ"שֶׁתַּצִּילֵנִי הַיּוֹם וּבְכָל יוֹם
מֵעַזֵּי פָנִים וּמֵעַזּוּת פָּנִים,
מֵאָדָם רַע, וּמֵחָבֵר רַע
וּמִשָּׁכֵן רַע", הִתְפַּלֵּל הַסָּב.
רַק כַּאֲשֶׁר עָבְרוּ עַל נַפְשִׁי
הַמַּיִם הַשְּׁחוֹרִים
וְתָלְשׁוּ אֶת עֲלֵי-הַכּוֹתֶרֶת מִתִּקְווֹתַי,
עָנִיתִי אָמֵן לְסָבִי שֶׁבְּגַן-עֵדֶן.

בְּעִיר אַחֶרֶת, לְיַד צְמָחִים אֲחֵרִים,
בְּעֶרֶב פֶּסַח,
כַּאֲשֶׁר שָׂרְפוּ אֶת הֶחָמֵץ
בְּכָל הַחֲצֵרוֹת
וּרְסִיס שֶׁל פִּיחַ הִתְעוֹפֵף
וְהִכְתִּים אֶת שִׂמְלָתָהּ,

The Bad Neighbor → *Tradition*

My grandfather used to pray,
"…and not into temptation, and not into disgrace…"
but the martyrs who died for the sake of God's name
sang in the sea:
"Temptation is a crown of blood,
a crown of royalty."
In unstained childhood, I listened to their song
with a terrible longing,
wildly fending off the timid, domestic prayers
that fled, trembling, from lightning and storms.

Those who died in the Holocaust

And, *"Save me today and every day*
from the insolent and from insolence,
from a bad person, and from a bad companion,
and from a bad neighbor," prayed my grandfather.
Only when the black waters crashed over my soul,
tearing the petals from my hopes,
did I answer "Amen" to my grandfather in paradise.

Crown of inheritance

In another city, beside other plants,
on the morning before Passover,
when the last of the bread
was being burned in all the yards
and a flake of ash flew up
and stained her dress,

הִיא זָנְקָה אֵלַי
בְּטַעֲנָה נִמְהָרָה כְּבָרָק,
בִּדְמָעוֹת:
"אַתְּ הָעוֹמֶדֶת שָׁם מִנֶּגֶד" –
צָעֲקָה,
"אֵינֵךְ דּוֹאֶגֶת לִי,
לְבוּשַׁי הַשְׁחִיר וְאֵינֵךְ אוֹמֶרֶת כְּלוּם!
הַבִּיטִי בִּי –
אֲנִי חוֹלָה, חוֹלָה מְאֹד וּמְלֵאָה יֵאוּשׁ".

טַעֲנָה תִּמְהוֹנִית
בְּפִי נְשָׁמָה שֶׁתְּמוֹל
שָׂכְרָה פֹּה חֶדֶר.
טַעֲנָה זָרָה, עַזָּה, רַעֲנַנָּה.
עָמֹק עָמֹק בְּתוֹכִי נָשְׁקָה נַפְשִׁי
אֶת שִׁגָּעוֹן כְּמִיהָתָהּ לָרֹד,
כְּמִיהָה מְפַקֶּרֶת, פּוֹרַעַת חֹק,
כְּמִיהָה הוֹרֶסֶת כְּרַעַשׁ אֲדָמָה.

פִּיהָ הָיָה גֵּיהִנּוֹם –
בְּפָתְחָהּ אֶת הַדֶּלֶת נֶחְבְּאוּ הַיְלָדִים
וְחָמְקוּ פְּנִימָה שְׁכֵנוֹת, שְׁכֵנִים.
צְחוֹקָהּ הַקַּר רָדַף אַחַר
קִיּוּמֵנוּ הַמְהֻגָּן, הַזּוֹרֵחַ בְּאוֹר
שִׁבְעַת הַיָּמִים;

she pounced on me, in tears,
with an accusation swift as lightning—
"You, standing there, across the way,"
she shouted,
"You don't care about me.
My clothes are blackened and you don't say a thing!
Look at me—
I am sick, very sick, and full of despair."

An astonishing accusation
from someone who only yesterday
rented a room here.
A bizarre claim, bold, fresh.
Deep within me, my soul kissed
the insanity of her longing for tenderness—
a lawless, unbridled longing,
destructive as an earthquake.

Her mouth was hell.
When she opened the door,
the children went into hiding,
and neighbors—women and men—
disappeared back into their houses.
Her cold laugh pursued our respectable existence,
which shone with the light of the seven days.

49

– אַל תִּדַּמּוּ בְּנַפְשְׁכֶם כִּי טוּבְכֶם
הוּא הַטּוֹב הָאֲמִתִּי,
צְוַח הַצְּחוֹק הַפִּרְאִי,
– אַל תִּדַּמּוּ בְּנַפְשְׁכֶם
כִּי תְפִלַּתְכֶם הִיא הַתְּפִלָּה הָאֲמִתִּית,
– אַל תִּדַּמּוּ בְּנַפְשְׁכֶם כִּי אֲדִיבוּתְכֶם
הִיא הָאֲדִיבוּת הָאֲמִתִּית,
– אַל תִּדַּמּוּ בְּנַפְשְׁכֶם כִּי שִׂמְחַתְכֶם
הִיא הַשִּׂמְחָה הָאֲמִתִּית,
– וְאַל תִּדַּמּוּ בְּנַפְשְׁכֶם כִּי אָשְׁרְכֶם
הוּא הָאֹשֶׁר הָאֲמִתִּי.
כַּאֲשֶׁר נוֹדַע
שֶׁהִיא נָסְעָה לְעִיר אַחֶרֶת,
כִּי הַסּוּפָה עָבְרָה וְאֵינֶנָּה,
נָשַׁמְנוּ לִרְוָחָה, פָּתַחְנוּ חַלּוֹנוֹת.
הַכּוּ הִכּוּ בַּתֻּפִּים,
תִּקְעוּ בַּשּׁוֹפָרוֹת,
עֲלֵי עָשׂוֹר וַעֲלֵי נָבֶל.
עַתָּה יוּנַח לָנוּ.
הַצִּיעוּ הַמִּטּוֹת,
הַלַּיְלָה נִישַׁן.
כַּאֲשֶׁר רָאִיתִי נְקֻדּוֹת-זָהָב
בְּעֵינֵי הָעֵדֶר –
מָלְאוּ כְּסָלַי בְּדִידוּת,
יָדַעְתִּי
כִּי דִבַּרְנוּ עַל נִשְׁמָתָהּ הַחַיָּה

"Don't imagine that your goodness
is genuine goodness,"
the savage laughter shrieked.
"Don't imagine
that your prayer is authentic prayer.
Don't imagine that your courtesy
is true courtesy,
or that your joy
is real joy,
or your happiness
genuine happiness."

When we heard that she had left for another city,
that the storm had passed and was gone,
we breathed deep and opened the windows.
Beat, beat the drums!
Blow the ram's horn!
Play the lyre and the harp!
Now we will be left in peace.
Make the beds, tonight we will sleep.
But when I saw the flecks of gold
in the eyes of the flock,
my heart filled with loneliness.
I knew that we had been speaking
of her living soul,

הַנִּשְׂרֶפֶת יוֹם־יוֹם,
כְּעַל אֶבֶן־נֶגֶף.
לַשָּׁוְא פָּרְשׂוּ קְלָלוֹתֶיהָ
יָדַיִם עֲשֵׁנוֹת
לְחַבֵּק אֶת נִשְׁמוֹתֵינוּ הַפּוֹשְׂרוֹת
חֲסָרוֹת הַדִּמְיוֹן.
לַשָּׁוְא נוֹפְפָה אוֹתָהּ עֲלוּבָה
לְפָנַי בִּדְגָלֶיהָ הָאֲדֻמִּים, הַקְּרוּעִים,
כְּדֵי שֶׁאֵצֵא מֵעִגּוּל יְשׁוּתִי הַקָּסוּם
לְגַלּוֹת אֶת נְקֻדַּת קִיּוּמָהּ.
הָיִיתִי לְאַחַת מִן הַשְּׁחוֹחוֹת,
לְאַחַת מֵהֲמוֹן אֲפֹרוֹת הָרֹאשׁ,
לֹא נוֹתַר בִּי שָׂרִיד
מִן הָאֱמֶץ הַהוּא הַנֶּהְדָּר.

which burned day by day,
as though it were a stumbling block.
In vain had her curses
spread their smoking arms
to embrace our tepid souls,
empty of all imagination.
In vain had that wretched one
waved before my face
her torn, red flags
to draw me out of the enchanted circle
of my being
that I might discover the core
of her existence.
I had become one of the bowed women,
one of the crowd of gray-headed women,
not a trace left within me
of that marvelous courage.

memory of
that
challenge

מוֹל הַיָּם

כַּאֲשֶׁר שִׁחְרַרְתִּי אֶת דַּג הַזָּהָב
צָחַק הַיָּם
וְאִמֵּץ אוֹתִי
אֶל לִבּוֹ הֶחָפְשִׁי,
אֶל לִבּוֹ הַזּוֹרֵם.
אָז שַׁרְנוּ יַחַד
(אֲנִי וָהוּא):
לֹא תָמוּת נַפְשִׁי. הֲיִשְׁלֹט רָקָב
בְּזֶרֶם חַי?
הוּא שָׁר כָּךְ
עַל נַפְשׁוֹ הַסּוֹאֶנֶת,
וְאָנֹכִי שַׁרְתִּי
עַל נַפְשִׁי הַכּוֹאֶבֶת.

54

Facing the Sea

When I set free
the golden fish,
the sea laughed
and held me close
to his open heart,
to his streaming heart.
Then we sang together,
he and I:
"My soul will not die.
Can decay rule
a living stream?"
So he sang
of his clamoring soul
and I sang
of my soul in pain.

הירח מלמד תנ"ך

הַיָּרֵחַ מְלַמֵּד תַּנַּ"ךְ.
רַקֶּפֶת כַּלָּנִית וָהָר
מַקְשִׁיבִים בְּשִׂמְחָה.
רַק הַיַּלְדָּה בּוֹכָה.
כַּלָּנִית אֶת בִּכְיָהּ לֹא תִּשְׁמַע,
כַּלָּנִית לוֹהֶטֶת בַּתּוֹרָה,
כַּלָּנִית בּוֹעֶרֶת כְּפָסוּק.
רַקֶּפֶת לַבְּכִי לֹא תַּקְשִׁיב
רַקֶּפֶת מִתְעַלֶּפֶת
מִמְּתִיקוּת הַסּוֹד.
הָהָר אֶת בִּכְיָהּ לֹא יִשְׁמַע,
הָהָר שָׁקַע
בְּמַחֲשָׁבוֹת.

אַךְ הִנֵּה בָּא
הָרוּחַ הָרַךְ, הַמְבֻשָּׂם,
לָתֵת כָּבוֹד לַתִּקְוָה,
לָשִׁיר כָּל לֵב פָּרָשׁ מְעוֹפֵף,
צַיִד נִלְהָב,
הִנָּשֵׂא אֶל קַצְוֵי יָם.

Moon Is Teaching Bible

anyone can teach the Bible

Moon is teaching Bible.
Cyclamen, Poppy, and Mountain
listen with joy.
Only the girl cries.
Poppy can't hear her crying—
Poppy is blazing in Torah,
Poppy is burning like the verse.
Cyclamen doesn't listen to the crying—
Cyclamen swoons
from the sweetness of the secret.
Mountain won't hear her crying—
Mountain is sunk
in thought.

But here comes Wind,
soft and fragrant,
to honor hope, to sing
the heart of each flying rider,
each ardent hunter
swept to the ends of the sea.

flowers

→ red flower a really into the word of God

→ into the revelations of reading

→ grounded = deep into what is going

→ the wind is "winding"

*blown away by Bible... drowns out desire a regulates emotions

בנחל אכזב

בְּנַחַל אַכְזָב
הַחֵשֶׁק הַיָּחֵף
מֵרִיעַ לַשָּׁרָב
בַּחֲצוֹצְרָה שֶׁל פָּז.

מִשְׁתּוֹלֵל הַשָּׁרָב,
הַשֶּׁמֶשׁ יִשַּׁק.
הֶחְשִׁיךְ הָעוֹלָם
בְּלָעֵנוּ אָבָק.

רַק הַיַּסְמִין בָּאֹפֶל
יַלְבִּין
וְעֵינוֹ שֶׁל קַיִן
מִזְרֶה אֵשׁ.
נָשִׁים מִתְעַלְּפוֹת מֵרֵיחַ מָתוֹק,
מִפַּחַד חַם.

In the Dry Riverbed

In the dry riverbed
barefoot desire
trumpets to the heat wave
with a horn of gold.

The heat wave goes wild,
kisses the sun.
The world darkens,
dust swallows us up.

Only the jasmine
whitens in the dark,
and Cain's eye flashes fire.
Women faint from sweet scents
and hot fear.

רע לי מתי אמות

רַע לִי מָתַי אָמוּת.
מַשָּׂא כָּבֵד כְּסִילוּתִי,
מַשָּׂא כָּבֵד הָרֹךְ.
לַשָּׁוְא יְנַשֵּׁק אֶת עֵינַי
רוּחַ הַיָּם,
וִיפַנְקוּנִי בִּדְבַשׁ וּבְמֹר
עִשְׂבֵי הַכַּרְמֶל.
לְתִקְווֹת הַשֶּׁמֶשׁ אָבוּז –
וּלְהַבְטָחוֹת נִצָּנִים.

All This Misery— When Will I Die?

All this misery— When will I die?
My folly—a heavy burden;
tenderness—a heavy burden.
In vain, the sea wind kisses my eyes
and the grasses of Mount Carmel
pamper me with honey and myrrh.
I scorn the hopes of the sun
and the promises of blossoms.

שלומי

שְׁלוֹמִי קָשׁוּר בְּחוּט
אֶל שְׁלוֹמְךָ.

וְהַחַגִּים הָאֲהוּבִים
וּתְקוּפוֹת הַשָּׁנָה הַנִּפְלָאוֹת
עִם אוֹצַר הָרֵיחוֹת, הַפְּרָחִים,
הַפְּרִי, הֶעָלִים וְהָרוּחוֹת,
וְעִם הָעֲרָפֶל וְהַמָּטָר,
הַשֶּׁלֶג הַפִּתְאֹמִי
וְהַטַּל,
תְּלוּיִים עַל חוּט הַכְּמִיהָה.

אֲנִי וְאַתָּה וְהַשַּׁבָּת.
אֲנִי וְאַתָּה וְחַיֵּינוּ
בַּגִּלְגּוּל הַקּוֹדֵם.
אֲנִי וְאַתָּה
וְהַשֶּׁקֶר.
וְהַפַּחַד.
וְהַקְּרָעִים.
אֲנִי וְאַתָּה
וּבוֹרֵא הַשָּׁמַיִם שֶׁאֵין לָהֶם
חוֹף.
אֲנִי וְאַתָּה
וְהַחִידָה.
אֲנִי וְאַתָּה
וְהַמָּוֶת.

My Peace

My peace is tied by a thread
to yours.

And the beloved holidays
and glorious seasons of the year—
with the wealth of fragrances, flowers,
fruit, leaves, and winds,
the fog and the rain,
the sudden snow
and the dew—
are suspended on a thread of longing.

I and you and the Sabbath.
I and you and our lives
in the last incarnation.
I and you
and the lie.
And the fear.
And the breaches.
I and you
and the Creator
of the heavens that have no shore.
I and you
and the riddle.
I and you
and death.

צמח זר

בַּחֲצוֹת דָּלַק נֵר
בְּלִבּוֹ שֶׁל פֶּרַח
אָדֹם כַּדָּם.
בַּחֲצוֹת נִגַּר כַּזָּהָב
עַל אֵבֶל פָּנַי
חַגּוֹ שֶׁל צֶמַח זָר.

Strange Plant

At midnight, a candle glowed
in the heart
of a blood-red flower.
At midnight, on the grief
of my face,
a strange plant's celebration
streamed like gold.

כל שושנה

כָּל שׁוֹשַׁנָּה הִיא אִי
שֶׁל הַשָּׁלוֹם הַמֻּבְטָח,
הַשָּׁלוֹם הַנִּצְחִי.

בְּכָל שׁוֹשַׁנָּה מִתְגּוֹרֶרֶת
צִפּוֹר סַפִּירִית
שֶׁשְּׁמָהּ "וְכִתְּתוּ".

וְנִדְמֶה
כֹּה קָרוֹב
אוֹר הַשּׁוֹשַׁנָּה,
כֹּה קָרוֹב
נִיחוֹחָהּ,
כֹּה קָרוֹב
שֶׁקֶט הֶעָלִים,
כֹּה קָרוֹב
אוֹתוֹ אִי –
קַח סִירָה
וַחֲצֵה אֶת יָם הָאֵשׁ.

Each Rose

Each rose is an island
of the promised peace,
the eternal peace.

In each rose dwells
a sapphire bird
whose name is
"They shall beat their swords..."

And the light of the rose
seems so near,
and its fragrance
so near,
and the silence of the leaves
so near,
that island
so near—
take a boat
and cross the sea of fire.

עמדתי בירושלים

עָמַדְתִּי
בִּירוּשָׁלַיִם
הַתְּלוּיָה עַל עָנָן,
בְּבֵית־הַקְּבָרוֹת
עִם אֲנָשִׁים בּוֹכִים,
עֵץ עָקֹם.
הָרִים מְטֻשְׁטָשִׁים
וּמִגְדָּל.
הֲלֹא אֵינְכֶם!
דִּבֵּר אֵלֵינוּ
הַמָּוֶת.
הֲלֹא אֵינֶךָ!
הוּא פָּנָה אֵלַי.

עָמַדְתִּי
בְּתוֹךְ יְרוּשָׁלַיִם
הַמְשֻׁבֶּצֶת בַּשֶּׁמֶשׁ
הַמְחַיֶּכֶת כְּמוֹ כַּלָּה
בַּשָּׂדֶה
עַל יַד עֵשֶׂב דַּק וְיָרֹק.

מַדּוּעַ פָּחַדְתְּ מִמֶּנִּי אֶתְמוֹל בַּגֶּשֶׁם?
דִּבֵּר אֵלַי הַמָּוֶת.
הֲלֹא אֲנִי אָחִיךְ
הַשָּׁקֵט וְהַגָּדוֹל.

I Stood in Jerusalem

I stood
in Jerusalem—
Jerusalem suspended
from a cloud—
in the graveyard
with people weeping
and a crooked tree.
Blurred mountains
and a tower.
"You are not,"
Death spoke to us.
"You are not,"
he turned to me.

I stood
in the midst of Jerusalem—
Jerusalem bejeweled in the sun,
smiling like a bride—
in the field
beside slender green grass.

"Why were you afraid of me
yesterday in the rain?"
Death spoke to me.
"Am I not your quiet
older brother?"

אז תצעק נשמתי

אָז תִּצְעַק נִשְׁמָתִי:
שְׂפָתַיִם חֲרוּכוֹת
אַתֶּן בְּצַד אֶחָד
וְהָעוֹלָם בַּצַד הַשֵּׁנִי
וְכָל הָעוֹלָם בַּצַד הַשֵּׁנִי

כִּי
בְּאוֹתוֹ חֶדֶר מוּצָף שֶׁמֶשׁ
עָמַדְתִּי
כֹּה קָרוֹב אֵלֶיהָ
שֶׁפִּי נָגַע בְּפָנֶיהָ
אֲשֶׁר שָׁנוּ בְּחֶבְלֵי מָוֶת.
הִיא בִּטְּאָה אֶת שְׁמִי
בְּקוֹל
שֶׁלָּן עַל קַרְקַע הַיָּם,
בְּקוֹל רָחוֹק וּמְעַמְעָם
שֶׁנִּפֵּץ לִרְסִיסִים אֶת מַרְאוֹת
הַכֶּסֶף
אוֹתָתוּ אֶת שְׁמִי
שְׂפָתֶיהָ הֶעָשֵׁנוֹת.

Then My Soul Cried Out

Then my soul cried out—
"Scorched lips,
you are on one side,
the world on the other,
the whole world on the other side."

all the universe

For in that room
flooded with sun,
I stood so close to her
that my mouth touched her face,
which had changed in the throes of death.
She spoke my name
in a voice
that dwelt on the floor of the sea;
in a distant, muffled voice
that shattered to bits
the silver mirrors,
her smoldering lips
spelled out my name.

shattered / ripped
photos or memories. ?
↓
Selfish ?

Cursed ?

גירשתי מלבי

גֵּרַשְׁתִּי מִלִּבִּי
אֶת כָּל הַמִּלִּים
כִּי פָּנָה יוֹם
וְאִמִּי נִרְדְּמָה –
וְאִמִּי תִּישַׁן
עַד בּוֹא
הַמָּשִׁיחַ.

I Banished from My Heart

I banished all the words
from my heart
for the day had passed
and my mother drifted off,
and my mother will sleep
until Messiah comes.

פְּנַאי

הָיָה לָנוּ אוֹצָר סָמוּי שֶׁל פְּנַאי
עָדִין כַּאֲוִיר הַבֹּקֶר,
פְּנַאי שֶׁל סִפּוּרִים, דְּמָעוֹת, נְשִׁיקוֹת
וְחַגִּים.
פְּנַאי שֶׁל אִמָּא, סַבְתָּא, וְהַדּוֹדוֹת
יוֹשְׁבוֹת בְּנַחַת בְּסִירָה
שֶׁל זִיו,
שָׁטוֹת אַט־אַט
בְּדוּגִית הַשָּׁלוֹם
עִם הַיָּרֵחַ וְעִם הַמַּזָּלוֹת.

Leisure

We had a hidden treasure of leisure
delicate as morning air,
leisure of stories, kisses, tears,
leisure of holidays.
Leisure of mama, grandma, and the aunts
gliding in a boat of light,
slowly floating
in the small boat of peace
with the moon and the heavenly bodies.

מִשִּׁירֵי הַיַּלְדוּת

הָיִיתִי פַּרְפַּר
שֶׁהוּא אִי־עֲשִׂיָּה
שֶׁהוּא אִי־קֶבַע
שֶׁהוּא מַלְכוּת.
הָלוֹךְ הָלְכוּ
שְׁנוֹתַי הָרַכּוֹת
לְבַקֵּשׁ מְתִיקוּת
וּפָגְעוּ בְּשָׁרְשֵׁי הַיָּם.

הוֹי! הוֹי! הוֹי!
אָבִי וְאִמִּי
בּוֹכִים עַל הַחוֹף.

לָמָּה הַבְּכִי?
לָמָּה הַהִי?
הֲלֹא קַרְקַע הַיָּם
מֶרְכָּבָה לֵאלֹהִים.

From the Songs of Childhood

I was a butterfly—
a non-doing,
an impermanence,
royalty.
My tender years went forth
in search of sweetness,
and struck the roots of the sea.

Ai! Ai! Ai!
Father and Mother
weep on the shore.

Why the weeping?
Why the grief?
Surely the floor of the sea
is a chariot to God.

II

היכל האל-ינאה

The Invisible Carmel

1971

הכרמל האי־נראה

כַּאֲשֶׁר אָמוּת
לַעֲבֹר לְמַהוּת אַחֶרֶת –
יִפָּרֵד הַכַּרְמֶל הָאִי־נִרְאֶה
שֶׁהוּא כֻּלּוֹ שֶׁלִּי,
כֻּלּוֹ תַּמְצִית הָאשֶׁר,
שֶׁמְּחָטָיו, אִצְטְרֻבָּלָיו, פְּרָחָיו וַעֲנָנָיו
חֲקוּקִים בִּבְשָׂרִי –
מִן הַכַּרְמֶל הַנִּרְאֶה
עִם שְׁדֵרַת הָאֳרָנִים שֶׁיּוֹרֶדֶת לַיָּם.

הַאִם תַּעֲנוּג הַשְּׁקִיעָה הָאֲדֻמָּה
הוּא מִיסוֹד הַתְּמוּתָה שֶׁבִּי?
וְתַעֲנוּג הַבְּשָׂמִים
וְרֶגַע עַרְפְלֵי הַמַּיִם
וְרֶגַע הַשִּׁיבָה
לַמַּבָּט הַתַּקִּיף שֶׁל שְׁמֵי יְרוּשָׁלַיִם,
לָעֶלְיוֹן עַל הַכֹּל –
הַאִם מִיסוֹד הַתְּמוּתָה הוּא?

The Invisible Carmel

When I die
to become another essence,
the invisible Mount Carmel—
which is all mine, all
the quintessence of joy,
whose needles, cones, flowers, and clouds
are carved into my flesh—
will part from the visible Carmel
with its boulevard of pine trees
descending to the sea.

Does the pleasure of a red sunset
come from the mortal element in me?
And the pleasure of earth's perfumes,
and the moment when the sea bursts into spray,
and the moment of return
to the stern gaze of Jerusalem's sky,
to the Supreme One—
is all this from the mortal element?

＊

בְּעֵינָיו הָיוּ שָׂרוֹת
צִפֳּרֵי גַּן־עֵדֶן
וְנוֹצוֹת שֶׁל זָהָב נָשְׁרוּ
עַל הַסְּפָרִים.

אַךְ אֲנִי חָשַׁבְתִּי בִּקְפִּידָה יַלְדוּתִית:
הַשְּׂחוֹק אֵינוֹ הָגוּן
לְבַעַל זָקָן,
אֵינוֹ הָגוּן לְבַעַל הֲלָכָה –
אֵינוֹ הָגוּן לְאָב.

*

In his eyes, birds of paradise
were singing
and gold feathers drifted
onto the books.

But with childish strictness
I thought:
Laughter isn't proper
for a bearded man,
for a pious man,
for a father.

בתור הילדות פרי חדש

הַכִּרְכָּרָה מִדַּרְדֶּרֶת –
אַךְ אֵין בְּכֹחָם לְהַצִּילֵנִי מִלַּיְלָה רִאשׁוֹן
בְּהָרֵי יְרוּשָׁלַיִם,
לַיְלָה אֵינְסוֹפִי שֶׁנָּטַל מִן הַנְּשָׁמָה
אֶת תַּאֲוַת הַקִּנְיָן –
כַּאֲשֶׁר הַחֹשֶׁךְ הַמַּרְהִיב בָּלַע הָרִים
וַחֲצֵרוֹת, שִׂיחִים וְאִילָנוֹת,
וְהַסּוּסִים פָּסְעוּ עַל־פְּנֵי הַשָּׁמַיִם
עִם הַמַּזָּלוֹת.

כַּמֶּהָה הָיִיתִי לַחֲסוֹת
אַךְ אָבִי וְאִמִּי בָּכוּ בַּהֵיכָל הֶחָשׁוּךְ.
נִלְחַצְתִּי אֲלֵיהֶם –
אַךְ הֵם שָׁרוּ בְּאֵין קוֹל
"מָה אֱנוֹשׁ כִּי תִזְכְּרֶנּוּ".

וְהֵיכָן הָיָה סָבָא?
בְּהִתְנוֹצֵץ הַזְּרִיחָה כַּאֲשֶׁר שָׁתִינוּ יַיִן עַתִּיק
(לְיַד הַחַלּוֹנוֹת הַפְּתוּחִים)
שֶׁהֵבִיא לָנוּ אֲוִיר נָדִיב כַּיָּם
וּנְטוּל מַמָּשׁוּת –
נָטַשׁ סָבִי אוֹתָנוּ כִּי כָּלְתָה נַפְשׁוֹ

New Fruit in the Season of Childhood

The cart rolls downhill—
But they cannot save me from a first night
in the mountains of Jerusalem,
an endless night that stripped my soul
of material hunger,
when the spectacular darkness
swallowed mountains and courtyards,
bushes and trees,
and the horses stepped on the surface of the sky
with the constellations.

I longed for protection
but my father and mother wept in the dark chapel.
I pressed close to them
but they sang voicelessly,
"What is man that You should remember him?"

And where was Grandfather?
In the gleam of the sunrise
by the open windows,
while we drank old wine
that brought us air as noble as the sea
and devoid of reality—
my grandfather abandoned us
because his soul yearned

אֶל בְּנוֹ שֶׁבְּגַן־עֵדֶן.
וּבְעוֹד אִמִּי יוֹשֶׁבֶת עַל שַׁרְפְּרַף הָאֲבֵלִים
בְּטֶרֶם רָחַצְנוּ אֶת פָּנֵינוּ מִן הַדְּמָעוֹת
חָלָה אָבִי וְלֹא קָם מֵחָלְיוֹ.

לְיַד גָּדֵר הָאֲבָנִים הַהֲרוּסָה שׂוֹחֲחוּ בְּלַחַשׁ
הַמַּלְאָכִים שֶׁמְּמֻנִּים עַל הַטַּל עִם הָאִישׁ הֶעָיֵף
כַּאֲשֶׁר קָרַעְתִּי שִׂמְלָתִי הַדַּקָּה
לְסַמֵּן בְּאוֹת אֵבֶל אֶת יַלְדוּתִי
כַּאֲשֶׁר אִמִּי הַמְהַסֶּסֶת נֶעֶזְבָה בַּחֶדֶר הַנִּדָּח
שֶׁכְּתָלָיו מְסֻיָּדִים,
כַּאֲשֶׁר בְּכִיָהּ אָבַד בֵּין הֶהָרִים.

צִפּוֹר אֲפֹרָה בִּלְתִּי צְפוּיָה
שֶׁבָּאָה לֶאֱכֹל לֶחֶם,
הֵפִיצָה נֹגַהּ רְקִיעִים
וְדִמְעוֹת עֵינֵינוּ הִתְעָרְבְּבוּ
בְּאוֹר הַשְׁקִיעָה,
נִבְלְלוּ בַּפְאֵר הַכָּתֹם.
צִפּוֹר קַלִּילָה פִּתְאֹמִית

for his son in paradise.
And while my mother still sat
on the mourners' bench,
before we had washed our faces of tears,
my father grew sick
and did not recover from his illness.

By the wrecked fence of stones,
the angels in charge of the dew
talked in a whisper with the tired man—
while I tore my thin dress
to mark my childhood
with a sign of mourning;
while my hesitant mother was left
in the forsaken room with whitewashed walls;
while her weeping was lost
among the mountains.

An unexpected gray bird
who came for bread
radiated a heavenly brightness,
and the tears of our eyes mingled
with the light of the sunset,
blending with the orange splendor.
A light, sudden bird

הֵכִינָה אֶת נַפְשִׁי לִקְרַאת נִגּוּן הָעֲשָׂבִים
לִקְרַאת רֵיחַ הַתְּהִיָּה שֶׁל עֲצֵי הַזַּיִת
לִקְרַאת שִׂמְחַת הָעֲנָנִים
וְהִבְהוּב מְכַתּוֹת הַזְּכוּכִית.

וְשַׂעֲרוֹת אִמִּי הוֹלְכוֹת וּמַלְבִּינוֹת
מִתַּחַת לַצָּעִיף,
כִּי אָבִי הַמְהֻרְהָר, הַנִּפְעָם, הַנִּבְדָּל –
יָשֵׁן בְּלֵב הָהָר,
כִּי אָבִי הַכֵּהֶה שֶׁחַיָּיו הָיוּ רְמָזִים שֶׁל זָהָב,
רְמָזִים בִּלְבַד – שָׁקוּף כָּל־כָּךְ,
יָשֵׁן בְּלֵב הָהָר הַמִּסְלָע.

הִיא מַבִּיטָה בְּאֵימָה אֶל הָאֹפֶק הַבּוֹעֵר
מֵחַלּוֹנֵנוּ הַמְסֹרָג –
חֲלוֹמוֹתֶיהָ יְשֵׂרוּהָ כְּמִיהָתָהּ יְסָרַתָּה.
בַּחוּץ מְרַחֲפֵי פַרְפַּר בְּהַשְׁקֵט
סָבִיב סָבִיב
בַּחוּץ זוֹרַחַת אֶבֶן הַשֹּׁהַם.
שְׁכוּרָה אֲנִי מִמְּחוֹל נִיחוֹחוֹת מְרִירִים
שֶׁל גִּבְעוֹלֵי הָהָר
וּמִן הַהֶכֵּרוּת עִם הַטַּעַם הֶעָנֹג

prepared my soul for the song of the grasses,
for the scent of the olive trees' amazement,
for the joy of the clouds
and the flickering of the glass shards.

And my mother's hair grows whiter
beneath the kerchief
because my pensive, troubled, solitary father
sleeps in the heart of the mountain,
because my dark father whose life was hints of gold—
only hints—
and who hoped so fervently,
sleeps in the heart of the rocky mountain.

From behind the barred window,
she stares in fear at the burning horizon.
Her dreams have made her suffer,
her longing has made her suffer.
Outside, a butterfly quietly hovers
around and around;
outside the onyx shines.
I am drunk with the dance of bitter scents
rising from the mountain's stems,
and from acquaintance
with the cool, delicate taste

הַקָּרִיר קִמְעָה שֶׁל עֲנָבִים שְׁקוּפִים כַּמַּיִם
וְזַכִּים כְּאַחְלָמָה,
כִּי בְּתוֹר הַיַּלְדוּת אֲכִילַת פְּרִי חָדָשׁ
פּוֹתַחַת לִפְנֵי הַנֶּפֶשׁ אֶת שַׁעֲרֵי גַּן־הָעֵדֶן,
זֶה שֶׁאֵין בּוֹ עֵץ הַדַּעַת וְהַנָּחָשׁ,
שֶׁכְּרוּבִים אֵינָם שׁוֹמְרִים לְפִתְחוֹ
בְּלַהַט הַחֶרֶב הַמִּתְהַפֶּכֶת,
כִּי בְּתוֹר הַיַּלְדוּת טָבַל דִּמְיוֹנִי
בִּדְבַשׁ הַכֵּהֶה שֶׁל פְּרִי הַתָּמָר,
זֶה שֶׁהַרְרֵי הַנְּחֹשֶׁת הֶאֱצִילוּ זִיוָם לִקְלִפָּתוֹ –
וְנִפְתְּחָה לְפָנַי חוֹמַת הַזָּהָב הָעֲגֻלָּה
שֶׁל הָרִמּוֹן,
וְנִכְנַסְתִּי אֶל אַרְמוֹן שֶׁל חַלּוֹנוֹת שְׁקוּפִים
וּמְזֹרָקוֹת יַיִן.

אֲבָל בְּשָׁעוֹת מְאֻחָרוֹת שֶׁל לַיְלָה
כַּאֲשֶׁר אִמִּי מְכַבָּה אֶת עֲשִׂירִית הַנֵּפֶט
אֲנַחְנוּ מוּטָלוֹת בַּחֹשֶׁךְ
עִם חֲפָצִים חִדְלֵי תַּבְנִית
שְׁכוּחוֹת וּכְמוֹ נְטוּלוֹת גַּשְׁמִיּוּת –
קִיּוּמֵנוּ תָּלוּי בְּקוֹלוֹת הַשְּׁכֵנִים
שֶׁמֵּעֵבֶר לַקִּיר.

of grapes, translucent as water
and clear as amethyst.
For in the season of childhood,
eating new fruit
opens before the soul the gates of paradise—
a paradise with no tree of knowledge
and no snake,
whose entrance the cherubs do not guard
with the fiery, ever-turning sword.
For in the season of childhood,
my imagination dipped
into the dark honey of the date tree's fruit,
upon whose skin the copper mountains
bestowed their radiance.
And the pomegranate's round wall of gold
opened before me,
and I entered the palace of transparent windows
and fountains of wine.

But in night's late hours
when my mother puts out the kerosene lamp,
we lie in the dark, amid the formless objects,
forgotten, as though emptied of substance,
our existence hanging on the voices of the neighbors
beyond the wall.

כַּאֲשֶׁר הֵם שׁוֹתְקִים
נֶאֱנָחוֹת מְחִלּוֹת הֶעָפָר,
כַּאֲשֶׁר הֵם שׁוֹתְקִים
פּוֹעֲרִים אֶת פִּיהֶם הַנְּקִיקִים,
כַּאֲשֶׁר הֵם שׁוֹתְקִים
שׁוֹמַעַת אֲנִי אֶת צַעֲדֵי עֲצוּב הָרוּחַ
שֶׁעוֹלֶה עַל הָהָר בַּחֹשֶׁךְ
שֶׁיּוֹרֵד מִן הָהָר בַּחֹשֶׁךְ
כִּי בַּחוּץ הַחֹשֶׁךְ אַחֵר אַחֵר
כִּי בַּחוּץ אֶפְשָׁר לֵילֵךְ בְּתוֹךְ גַּנִּים וּבְסִתָּנִים
אֲפֵלִים כְּבוֹרוֹת
עַל פִּי הַכּוֹכָבִים.
בְּאַפְלַת הַחֶדֶר הַדּוֹמֵם עֵינַיִם אֲיֻמּוֹת
לְטוּשׁוֹת,
הַלֵּב נִבְעָת וְאֵין דָּמָיו זָזִים –
מֵעֵבֶר לַקִּיר בָּאָה מִלָּה
הִיא מְגַשֶּׁשֶׁת בָּעֲלָטָה,
יָשַׁבְנוּ בְּתוֹכָהּ כְּמוֹ בְּתוֹךְ סִירָה
נִצַּלְנוּ.

When they are silent,
the tunnels of dust groan;
when they are silent,
the mouths of the crevices open;
when they are silent
I hear the steps
of the wind's sadness
rising up the mountain in the dark,
winding down the mountain in the dark.

For outside, the darkness is different,
completely different.
Outside one can walk
among gardens and orchards dark as pits,
guided by the stars.
In the darkness of the quiet room,
terrible eyes glare,
the heart is struck with fear,
its blood stops coursing—

From beyond the wall
came a word
groping in the deep darkness.
We sat within it as inside a boat,
rescued.

מָתַי הִתְחַלְּפוּ הַמַּלְכֻיּוֹת בַּגְּבָהִים
וְהָאוֹר הַטָּהוֹר נִכְנַס אֶל הַחֶדֶר הָאָבֵל
צְבָעִים לְהָעִיר וְצוּרוֹת –
מָתַי הֵקִיצוּ הָעֵינַיִם הַנּוֹצְצוֹת
שֶׁל בְּנֵי אָדָם?
וַאֲנִי הוֹדֶפֶת מֵעָלַי רֵיחוֹת בְּשׁוּל שְׁפוֹסְעִים
מִכָּל צַד,
כִּי מְטִילִים הֵם כְּתָמִים עַל הָרִקְמָה הַדַּקָּה
שֶׁל הִרְהוּרַי,
וַאֲנִי מַבִּיטָה עַל הַבָּנוֹת הַקְּטַנּוֹת שֶׁל הַשָּׁכֵן
עַל מְמָרְקוֹת אַבְנֵי הֶחָצֵר –
שָׁם פַּרְגּוֹד הַשַּׂקִּים נָטוּי כִּקְלָלָה
עַל דַּרְכֵי הַזְּרִיחוֹת,
מַבִּיט עַל חַיַּי בְּעֵינָיו הַקָּמוֹת.

אַט־אַט הִתְיַדַּדְתִּי עִם הַשָּׁמַיִם
וְהִתְחַלְתִּי לְהַבְחִין בֵּין חֹשֶׁךְ לְחֹשֶׁךְ
בֵּין לַיְלָה לְלַיְלָה
וְאָמַרְתִּי בְּלִבִּי:
שֵׁם הַלֵּילוֹת הַיְרֻקִּים הַשְּׁקוּפִים כַּיָּם –
"פִּתִּיתַנִי ה' וָאֶפָּת" אוֹ כֶּתֶר יִרְמְיָהוּ,
וְשֵׁם הַלֵּילוֹת הַכְּחֻלִּים, לֵילוֹת אוֹר הַכּוֹכָבִים –

When did the kingdoms in the heights change
and the pure light enter the mourner's room
to waken colors and forms—
when did the shining eyes
of human beings awaken?
I cast off the smells of cooking all around me
because they stain the thin embroidery
of my contemplations.
And I gaze at the neighbor's little daughters
as they polish the courtyard stones—
the burlap curtain spread out there like a curse
on the paths of the sunrises,
staring at my life with its blind eyes.

Slowly I befriended the sky
and began to distinguish
darkness from darkness,
night from night.
And I said to myself:
The name of the green nights,
transparent as the sea,
is *"You enticed me, God,*
and I was enticed"
or Jeremiah's crown.
And the name of the blue nights,

"בֵּאלֹהִים בָּטַחְתִּי לֹא אִירָא מַה־יַּעֲשֶׂה בָשָׂר לִי",
וַחֲלוֹם יַעֲקֹב הוּא לַיְלָה שֶׁל כֶּסֶף,
לַיְלָה שֶׁל לְבָנָה.

אַט־אַט הִתְחַלְתִּי לְהַבְחִין
בֵּין פָּנִים לְפָנִים, בֵּין קוֹל לְקוֹל
וְהַבָּנוֹת הַקְּטַנּוֹת נֶהֶפְכוּ לְשׁוֹשַׁנּוֹת לְבָנוֹת
וּלְשׁוֹשַׁנּוֹת שֶׁהֶעָלִים שֶׁלָּהֶן זָהָב.
הַשּׁוֹשַׁנּוֹת נִמְלָטוֹת מִן הָרֶשֶׁת הַגְּדוֹלָה
שֶׁפּוֹרֵשׂ הַחֹשֶׁךְ הַקַּדְמוֹן –
בִּרְחוֹבוֹת רֵיקִים וּבְסִמְטָאוֹת
הַשּׁוֹשַׁנּוֹת לוֹחֲשׁוֹת:
הַלְוַאי וְיַעֲמֹד אִישׁ לְיַד הַשַּׁעַר,
שֶׁבְּעֵינָיו דַּעַת הַשֶּׁמֶשׁ.

אִישׁ שֶׁפָּנָיו לְבָנוֹת כַּנִּיר
מַבִּיט בִּפְלִיאָה שֶׁעוֹלָה עַל גְּדוֹתֶיהָ
עַל הָעֲלָמוֹת הַקְּטַנּוֹת.
הוּא שָׁר לְפָנֵינוּ בְּקוֹלוֹ הַגּוֹוֵעַ
עַל הַמֶּלֶךְ רָם הַקּוֹמָה
עַל אֶצְבְּעוֹת הַגַּנִּים הָעֵרִים
עַל שַׁעֲרֵי הַנְּחֹשֶׁת שֶׁל בֵּית־הַחוֹלִים.

the nights of starlight—
"In God I trust,
I am not afraid,
what can mortals do to me?"
And Jacob's dream is a night of silver,
a night of moon.

Slowly I began to distinguish
face from face,
voice from voice,
and the little girls turned into white roses
and into roses with leaves of gold.
The roses flee from the great net
spread by the primeval darkness.
In empty streets and alleys, the roses whisper,
"If only a man would come to stand beside the gate
in whose eyes is the wisdom of the sun."

A man whose face is white as paper
gazes in overbrimming wonder
at the small young women.
He sings before us in a dying voice,
about the king, great in stature,
about the fingers of the blind players,
about the copper gates of the hospital.

הָאִישׁ הַחִוֵּר עוֹשֶׂה תַּכְשִׁיטִים
מִפְּסוּקִים עַתִּיקִים
וְשָׂם אוֹתָם בַּלַּיְלָה עַל רָאשֵׁי הֶהָרִים.

בַּבֹּקֶר אוֹמֶר לִי אַלְמֻת הַכֶּסֶף:
הָאִישׁ הַנִּלְעַג שֶׁשָּׂר לְפָנַיִךְ
קָרוֹב לִי בְּשֹׁרֶשׁ הַנֶּפֶשׁ.
בַּבֹּקֶר לִמְּדַנִי אַלְמֻת הַכֶּסֶף
לְהַבְחִין בֵּין יוֹם שֶׁל אֵשׁ לְבָנָה
לְיוֹם שֶׁל אֵשׁ צְהֻבָּה
בֵּין רְחוֹבוֹת הַשֶּׁמֶשׁ
לִרְחוֹבוֹת פְּסֹלֶת הַזָּהָב.

חַשְׁמַל מַחְשְׁבוֹתַי הַשּׁוֹרְקוֹת
כְּרוּחַ קָדִים
מַפְחִיד אֶת אִמִּי הָרַכָּה
הַסְּפוּנָה בַּבַּיִת
וְהִיא עוֹצֶמֶת אֶת עֵינֶיהָ
כְּדֵי שֶׁתּוּכַל לִבְכּוֹת
עַל צַוְּארֵי אָבִיהָ וְאִמָּהּ
שֶׁאֵין אֲלֵיהֶם שְׁבִיל בַּנִּגְלֶה.

The pale man makes jewelry
out of ancient verses
and sets it at night on the tops of the mountains.

In the morning, the flower called silver-everlasting
says to me,
 "The scorned man who sings before you
is close to the root of my soul."
In the morning, the silver-everlasting
teaches me
to distinguish between a day of white fire
and a day of yellow fire,
between streets of sun
and streets of the gold's dross.

The electricity of my thoughts,
whistling like a hot eastern wind,
frightens my tender mother
hidden in the house,
and she shuts her eyes, to cry
on the necks of her father and mother,
to whom there is no visible path.

הַשֶּׁמֶשׁ הֵאִירָה עָנָף לַח

הַשֶּׁמֶשׁ הֵאִירָה עָנָף לַח
וְעָלִים שֶׁל זָהָב צָדוּ
הָאִישׁוֹנִים;
עֲלֵי הַזָּהָב שֶׁנָּסְעוּ
לַיְלָה וָיוֹם
בְּתוֹךְ דַּם לִבִּי,
שִׁנּוּ תַּבְנִיתָם.

וְכַאֲשֶׁר הִגִּיעוּ
עַד הַנְּשָׁמָה
עַד בְּדִידוּתָהּ,
הָפְכוּ לְאוֹתוֹת רְחוֹקִים
שֶׁל אוֹר,
לִרְמָזִים מִשָּׁמַיִם
מוֹפָתִים עַתִּיקִים.

The Sun Lit a Wet Branch

The sun lit a wet branch
and gold leaves captured my eyes.
The gold leaves that coursed
night and day
through my heart's blood
changed their configuration.

And when they reached the soul,
its solitude,
they became distant signs
of light,
clues from heaven,
ancient wonders.

כי האור שעשועי

כַּאֲשֶׁר אַתָּה יוֹשֵׁב כְּמֶלֶךְ בַּשֶּׁבִי
וּמַבִּיט דּוּמָם עַל הָרְחוֹב הַסַּלְעִי
גּוֹאָה מְתִיקוּת בְּלִבִּי הַמְיַלֵּל
כַּאֲשֶׁר אַתָּה מַבִּיט עַל הַזָּר
הָעוֹבֵר שָׁם לְאִטּוֹ,
מִסַּעֲרַת אַבִּיט בָּאוֹר
מִסְתַּנֵּן מִבַּעַד לְעָלִים שֶׁל עֵץ הָאַגָּס
כִּי הָאוֹר שַׁעֲשׁוּעָי.

כַּאֲשֶׁר אֵינְךָ עִמָּדִי
כַּאֲשֶׁר הַבַּיִת רֵיק
מְשׁוֹטֶטֶת נַפְשִׁי בֶּחָלָל
מְנֻתֶּקֶת מִן הַמַּזָּל שֶׁשְּׁמוֹ אֶרֶץ
מְנֻתֶּקֶת מִן הָאַוִּיר הַשּׂוֹחֵק
מְנֻתֶּקֶת מִמַּיִם וַעֲיָנוֹת
מְנֻתֶּקֶת מִן הֶהָרִים וִיפִי הָאִילָנוֹת
מְנֻתֶּקֶת מֵחֹם הַחַיּוֹת
מְנֻתֶּקֶת מִקַּו הָעוֹפוֹת
מְנֻתֶּקֶת מֵהֶבֶל פִּי אָדָם
מְנֻתֶּקֶת מִן הָאוֹתִיּוֹת.

For the Light Is My Joy (1971)

When you sit like a king in captivity,
gazing silently at the rocky street,
a sweetness rises in my howling heart.
When you gaze at the stranger
slowly passing by,
I stare, restless, at the light
filtering through the leaves of the pear tree,
for the light is my joy.

Her dead husband

When you are not with me,
when the house is empty,
my soul wanders in space,
detached
from the planet we call earth
and from the laughing air,
from fountains
and from seas,
from mountains
and the beauty of trees,
from animal warmth
and the arc of the birds,
from human breath,
from words.

103

תְּמֵהָה אֲנִי כִּי שְׁנֵי אַנְשֵׁי הַחֲלָלִית
לֹא רָאוּ עַל פְּנֵי הַיְשִׁימוֹן הַזְּגוּגִי
שֶׁל הַלְּבָנָה
אֶת צִלּוֹ שֶׁל הַנָּבִיא יוֹנָה,
כִּי רַק לֵב שֶׁנָּטַשׁ אֶת הָעוֹלָם
שָׂמֵחַ כָּךְ לִידִידוּת הַקִּיקָיוֹן
רַק לֵב שָׁרוּי בִּישִׁימוֹן
מֵאֲשֶׁר בְּאֹרַח כָּזֶה
בַּחֻבָּה הָאִלֶּמֶת שֶׁל עָלִים
וּמְבַקֵּשׁ לָמוּת
כַּאֲשֶׁר מֵתִים צְמָחִים
אֲשֶׁר לֹא זָרַע.

יוֹנָה הַנָּבִיא שֶׁדַּרְכּוֹ אֶל אֱלֹהִים
מָלְאָה בְּרִיחוֹת
בְּתוֹךְ מַיִם זוֹעֲמִים
יְבַקֵּשׁ עָלֶיךָ רַחֲמִים
וְעָלַי
וְעַל כָּל הַטּוֹבְעִים.

I am amazed that the two astronauts
did not see the prophet Jonah's shadow
on the glassy wilderness of the moon.
For only a heart that has abandoned the world
delights this way
in the gourd tree's friendship,
only a heart that dwells in wilderness
contents itself like this
with the mute affection of leaves
and seeks to die
with the death of plants
it did not sow.

Jonah the prophet, whose path to God
was filled with flights through raging waters,
will ask mercy for you
and for me
and for all who are drowning.

Research : Jonah

Commentary

+Book of Jonah

אל תרחק

הַמְנַחֲמִים בָּאִים אֶל הֶחָצֵר
הַחִיצוֹנָה
עוֹמְדִים עַל יַד הַשַּׁעַר
אֲשֶׁר פָּנָיו אֶל גֵּיא צַלְמָוֶת
וְאֵימָתוֹ סָבִיב סָבִיב.
עֲמִידָה עַל יַד הַשַּׁעַר כָּל יְכָלְתָּם
שֶׁל מְנַחֲמִים לָשֵׂאת.
גַּם נַפְשִׁי בְּמֶרְחַק פַּרְסָאוֹת
מִן הָאֲנִי שֶׁל הַבּוֹכֶה. גְּזֵרָה הִיא.

יוֹצֵר לֵילוֹת וָרוּחַ
הֲלֹא נֶגְדְּךָ בְּכִי אִם זֶה,
אַל תִּרְחַק –
אַל יַעַמְדוּ כְּחַיִץ
מִילְיוֹנֵי שְׁנוֹת אוֹר
בֵּינְךָ וּבֵין אִיּוֹב.

Be Not Far

The consolers come
to the outer courtyard
and stand by the gate that faces
the valley of the shadow of death
with its terror all around.
Standing by the gate is all
they can bear to do.
My soul, too, is miles
from the I of the weeper.
Inevitably.

O Creator of nights and wind,
this terrible weeping is aimed at You—
be not far away.
Let not millions of light-years
stand like a barrier
between You and Job.

אַתָּה שׁוֹתֵק אֵלַי

אַתָּה שׁוֹתֵק אֵלַי
מִן הָעוֹלָם הֶכָּמוּס.
בָּלַע הָהָר אֶת כָּל הַמְּקוֹמוֹת
אֲשֶׁר הִתְהַלַּכְתָּ שָׁם חַי.
אֲנִי מְכַסֶּה אֶת שְׁתִיקָתְךָ
בָּאוֹתִיּוֹת וּבְקוֹלָם,
אֲנִי מְכַסֶּה אֶת הָאַיִן
בְּצִפֳּרִים שֶׁבָּאוֹת לִשְׁתּוֹת מַיִם,
וּבִנְחָשִׁים כֵּן בִּנְחָשִׁים.

לֹא הָיָה דָבָר אֲשֶׁר לֹא קְרָאתִיו
נֵר –
כִּי אֶפְחַד
פֶּן בַּחֹשֶׁךְ לֹא אַבְחִין
בֵּין מַיִם חַיִּים
לְבוֹרוֹת נִשְׁבָּרִים.

108

You Call Out Silence to Me

You call out silence to me
from the hidden world.
The mountain has swallowed all the places
where you once walked alive.
I cover up your silence
with the letters and their sounds,
I cover up the Nothingness
with birds that come to sip water
and with snakes,
yes, with snakes.

There is no thing
I have not called a candle—
for I fear that in the dark
I will not distinguish
living water from empty wells.

כַּאֲשֶׁר הָיִיתָ פֹּה

כַּאֲשֶׁר הָיִיתָ פֹּה
וּמַבָּטְךָ הַחוֹם מֵגֵן עָלַי
וּמַחְשְׁבוֹתֵינוּ נוֹגְעוֹת
פֶּתַע
כָּנָף אֶל כָּנָף.

כַּאֲשֶׁר הָיִיתָ עִמָּדִי
בְּתוֹךְ הַדְּבָרִים הַחוֹלְפִים
הָיוּ הַקִּירוֹת בְּנֵי-בַּיִת קְשִׁישִׁים
שֶׁסִּפְּרוּ מַעֲשִׂיּוֹת עַתִּיקוֹת
בָּעֶרֶב
כַּאֲשֶׁר שָׁתִינוּ תֵּה.

עַכְשָׁו הַקִּירוֹת אֵינָם מַחֲסֶה
הֵם הִסְתַּגְּרוּ בִּשְׁתִיקָתָם
וְלֹא יַשְׁגִּיחוּ בְּנָפְלִי
עַכְשָׁו הַקִּירוֹת סִיד וָמֶלֶט
יְסוֹד זָר
חֹמֶר לֹא עוֹנֶה כַּמָּוֶת.

When You Were Here

When you were here,
your brown glance protecting me
and our thoughts touching
suddenly
wing to wing,

when you were with me
among the passing things,
the walls were like elderly relations
telling ancient tales in the evenings
as we drank our tea.

Now the walls are no shelter.
Withdrawn into their own silence,
they pay no attention to my fall.
Now the walls are plaster and concrete,
a strange element,
matter
unresponsive as death.

*

אֲנִי בְּבֵיתִי שׁוֹכֶבֶת
וְהַיָּם מֵרָחוֹק מֵרָחוֹק
בַּחֹשֶׁךְ יַהֲלֹךְ.
הַשְׁאִירוּ מְעַט אוֹר
בִּי
אַל תַּעַשְׂקוּנִי יִסּוּרִים.

＊

I lie in my house,
and in the distant distance
the sea wanders through the dark.
Leave a bit of light
in me,
do not ravage me,
O sufferings.

} psalms : release

＊prayer to who?

דו־שִׂיחַ פְּרָאִי

דּו־שִׂיחַ פְּרָאִי
בֵּין אִשָּׁה בְּלוּלָה בְּצַעַר
וְהַשֶּׁמֶשׁ מִמַּעַל
בְּלָשׁוֹן עֲדִינָה רוֹטֶטֶת
שֶׁל קַרְנֵי הָאוֹר,
בְּסוֹד צִבְעֵי הַקֶּשֶׁת.
וְכַאֲשֶׁר הִיא עוֹצֶמֶת עֵינֶיהָ
פִּתְאֹם
בָּא לִקְרָאתָהּ נַחְשׁוֹל אָדֹם
וּמְכַסֶּה אֶת נוֹצוֹת הַטַּוָּס אֲשֶׁר צִיֵּר צִיֵּר הָאֲוִיר,
וְכַאֲשֶׁר הִיא עוֹצֶמֶת עֵינַיִם לֵאוֹת
בּוֹלֵעַ יָם אָפֵל
אֶת הָעוֹלָם.

Savage Dialogue

A savage dialogue
between a woman wrapped in grief
and the sun above
in the delicate, trembling tongue
of light rays,
in the secret
of the rainbow's colors—
And when she shuts her eyes,   *rejects light*
suddenly
a red torrent rushes towards her
and blots out the peacock's feathers   *Angery @ self*
painted by the air.   *bad luck?*
And when she shuts her weary eyes,
a dark sea swallows   *willingly going into*
the world.   *darkness*

III

ﬡ ﬡ ﬡ ﬡ

Be Not Far

1974

שושנה שחורה

הַאִם גַּעְגּוּעַי בָּרְאוּ
שׁוֹשַׁנָּה שְׁחוֹרָה שֶׁנָּתַתְּ לִי
בַּחֲלוֹם
אוֹ גַּעְגּוּעַיִךְ חָדְרוּ בִּדְמוּת פֶּרַח
מִן הָעוֹלָם הַכָּמוּס
אֶל חֲלוֹמִי.
וּמַדּוּעַ בְּקַשְׁתִּי מִמֵּךְ
פִּתְאֹם עֲגִילִים,
דָּבָר שֶׁלֹּא עָשִׂיתִי מֵעוֹלָם
כַּאֲשֶׁר הָיִיתְ בְּאֶרֶץ הַחַיִּים.

Black Rose

Did my longings create
the black rose that you gave me
in the dream,
or did your longings pierce my dream
in the form of a flower
from the hidden world?
And why did I suddenly
ask you for earrings,
something I never did
when you were in the land of the living?

כאשר בירכתי על הנרות

כַּאֲשֶׁר בֵּרַכְתִּי עַל הַנֵּרוֹת
קָרְאוּ כִּסוּפַי בְּקוֹל:
שַׁבָּת שָׁלוֹם, יַקִּירִי –
אַךְ הֵמָּה נָטְשׁוּ אֶת אַרְצוֹת הַחַיִּים
וְלֹא עָנוּ לָרֹד.

אָמַר חַגִּי הָרוֹעֵד: שָׁרָשַׁי לְמַעְלָה.
לָחַשְׁתִּי:
שָׁלוֹם לָךְ, שַׁבָּת לָךְ, נִשְׁמָתִי.

מִבַּעַד לְדִמְעוֹתַי שׁוֹטְטוּ שַׁלְהָבוֹת
וְהַבְקִיר כֻּלּוֹ זָהָב מְנַצְנֵץ,
כָּל־כָּךְ אוֹר מִסְּבִיבִי
וְכָל כָּךְ הַכְּאֵב –
עוֹד רֶגַע וְתֵצֵא נִשְׁמָתִי.

When I Said the Blessing over the Candles

When I said the blessing over the candles,
my yearnings called out,
"Good Sabbath to you, my dear ones."
But they had left the lands of the living
and did not respond to tenderness.

My trembling holiday said,
"My roots are above."
I whispered,
"Peace to you, Sabbath to you,
my soul."

Flames wander through my tears
and the wall shimmers gold.
So much light around me,
so great the pain—
one more moment, and my soul
will depart.

כאשר חי המלך

כַּאֲשֶׁר חַי הַמֶּלֶךְ
הָיָה כְּבוֹד בַּת הַמֶּלֶךְ
פְּנִימָה
בַּבַּיִת.
עַכְשָׁו הַבַּיִת רְסִיסִים רְסִיסִים.
כַּאֲשֶׁר חַי הַמֶּלֶךְ
הָיְתָה צְנִיעוּת
הָיָה חַג.
כַּאֲשֶׁר חַי הַמֶּלֶךְ
הָיְתָה הַשַּׁבָּת שׁוֹשַׁנִּים
עַכְשָׁו הִיא פֶּצַע.
כַּאֲשֶׁר חַי הַמֶּלֶךְ
הָיוּ הַמַּחֲשָׁבוֹת שֶׁבַּלֵּב
צִפֳּרִים
שֶׁהִתְעוֹפְפוּ בָּעֶרֶב,
שֶׁחִכּוּ לִמְנוּחַת הָעֶרֶב.
עַכְשָׁו חֲשׂוּפִים שָׁרָשַׁי
וַאֲנָשִׁים דּוֹרְכִים עֲלֵיהֶם.

When the King Was Alive

When the king was alive,
the glory of the princess
was within,
in the house.
Now the house is in shambles.
When the king was alive
there was modesty,
there was celebration.
When the king was alive,
the Sabbath was roses;
now it's a wound.
When the king was alive,
the heart's thoughts were birds
flying about in the evening,
waiting for evening's rest.
Now my roots are exposed
and people trample them.

אל תשליכני מלפניך

הִיא גָּחֲנָה אֶל נַפְשִׁי
לִנְגֹּעַ בַּבְּכִי שֶׁבִּגְרוֹנִי,
שׁוֹכֵן עַד –
נְגִיעָתָהּ עוֹשָׂה בִּי
קְרָעִים קְרָעִים.
קָשֶׁה לְלֵב אוֹבֵד
עִם חֲשֵׁכוֹת
וְעִם מִלִּים –

אַל תַּשְׁלִיכֵנִי מִלְּפָנֶיךָ

וְכַאֲשֶׁר אָקִיץ מֵחֲלוֹמִי
וְחֹשֶׁךְ יִהְיֶה סְבִיבִי
וְרָהִיטֵי הַיְשָׁנִים יַשְׁמִיעוּ
קוֹלוֹת נֶפֶץ דַּקִּים –

אַל תַּסְתִּיר פָּנֶיךָ מִמֶּנִּי.

כַּאֲשֶׁר אָקִיץ לְהַרְהֵר
הֲמָתְקוּ כָּל-כָּךְ הַסִּפּוּרִים
שֶׁמְּסַפְּרִים הַחוּשִׁים
לְנִשְׁמָתִי –
(הַאִם סִפּוּרִים מִבְּצָרַי?)
הֲלֹא בְּשָׁעָה אֲבֵלָה עֲשָׂנָה
בִּי נֹגַע בִּקְשִׁיחוּת שֶׁל מְלִיצָה
אַף יָפְיוֹ הָרַד שֶׁל פֶּרַח.

Cast Me Not Away

She leaned toward my soul
to touch the cry in my throat,
ever-dwelling—

Her touch tears me to pieces.
Darknesses and words
are difficult
for the heart that is lost—

Cast me not away from Your presence.

And when I wake from my dream,
surrounded by darkness,
the old furniture making
its thin creaking sounds—

Do not hide Your face from me.

When I wake, wondering
if the stories of my senses
are really so sweet to my soul—
(Are stories my fortress?)
Oh, at a mournful, smoldering hour
even the tender beauty of a flower
has touched me with the harshness of flattery.

כַּאֲשֶׁר אָקִיץ בּוֹכִיָּה
לוּ אֵדַע
לְאָן מוֹבִילִים אֶת חַיֵּי
הַשָּׁמַיִם.

When I wake, weeping—
if only I might know
where heaven is leading
my life.

החול הדק החול הנורא

אִם נַפְשִׁי עַל צִדָּהּ תִּשְׁכַּב
חֲפוּרָה בְּתוֹךְ צַעַר
וְנִרְתַּעַת מֵאַלִּימוּת
שֶׁבָּאֲנָשִׁים, בַּמְּכוֹנוֹת, וּבַנְּחָשִׁים,
וְלֹא תָשׁוּט בְּסֵתֶר הַלַּיְלָה
וְלֹא תָעוּף עִם רוּחַ דֶּרֶךְ עָלִים
קְרוּעָה מִטְּקָסֵי חַג
בְּלִי שְׁבִיל אֶל קוֹל חַי,

אִם נַפְשִׁי עַל צִדָּהּ תִּשְׁכַּב
וְלֹא תִשְׁמַע קוֹל חַם
אֶת שְׁמָהּ לוֹחֵשׁ,
הִיא תִּשְׁכַּח רַחֲמֵי הַשֶּׁמֶשׁ
וְחוֹמוֹת הֶהָרִים
וְאוֹתוֹ מַעְיָן חָבוּי
שֶׁשְּׁמוֹ דּוּ־שִׂיחַ
(מַעְיָן הֵאִיר בַּחֹשֶׁךְ).

אִם נַפְשִׁי עַל צִדָּהּ תִּשְׁכַּב
עֲטוּפָה בְּקוּרֶיהָ
מְגֹרֶשֶׁת מִמַּעֲשִׂים
מְסֻלֶּקֶת מִן הַיּוֹם־יוֹם
יָבוֹא מִשְׁפַּת הַיָּם
חוֹל דַּק
וִיכַסֶּה אֶת שַׁבְּתוֹתֶיהָ

The Fine Sand, the Terrible Sand

If my soul lies down on its side,
dug deep into sorrow,
recoiling from violence
in people, snakes, machines,
and does not sail in the secret of the night,
and does not fly through the leaves with the wind,
and is torn from ritual celebrations,
without a path to the living voice,

if my soul lies down on its side
and does not hear a warm voice
whispering its name,
it will forget the mercy of the sun
and the walls of the mountains
and that hidden spring whose name
is conversation
(a spring that once shone in the dark).

If my soul lies down on its side
wrapped in its webs,
divorced from deed,
expelled from the day-to-day,
a fine sand will come from the shore of the sea
and cover its Sabbaths,

וְיִסְתֹּם הֲגִיגִים עַד הַשֹּׁרֶשׁ.
אֶל מִסְתּוֹרִין בְּכִיָּה
לִפְנֵי יָהּ טָמִיר וְנֶעְלָם,
יַחְדֹּר הַחוֹל הַדַּק הַנּוֹרָא

אִם נַפְשִׁי עַל צִדָּהּ תִּשְׁכַּב חֲפוּרָה בְּצַעַר.

and block to the root its meditations.
The fine, terrible sand
will pierce the mystery of its weeping
before the veiled, hidden God

if my soul lies down on its side, dug deep in sorrow.

השמענה קולכן ברכות השחר

מַחֲשָׁבָה טוֹרֶדֶת
הֶחֱזִיקָה בְּכַף־יָדָהּ
אֶת רוּחִי
כָּל הַלַּיְלָה
וְלֹא יָכֹלְתִּי לְהֵרָדֵם –
צִפָּרְנֶיהָ קָרְעוּ אֶת הָרְשׁוּמִים
שֶׁל חֲלוֹמוֹתַי
וְטָבַעְתִּי
בְּרָחוֹק שֶׁל בּוֹרוֹת
מִן הָעוֹלָם.

כִּידִיד נֶפֶשׁ
שֶׁהַלֵּב הִתְיָאֵשׁ לִרְאוֹתוֹ
בְּאַרְצוֹת הַחַיִּים
הוֹפִיעַ הַבֹּקֶר.
בָּרוּךְ הַבָּא
בָּרוּךְ הַבָּא
הַמַּלְאָךְ הַגּוֹאֵל!
וְאֵיךְ מְחַכִּים לַזְּרִיחָה
הַחוֹלִים כַּאֲשֶׁר
מִתְהַפְּכִים הֵם
מִצַּד אֶחָד שֶׁל הַכְּאֵב
לְצַד אַחֵר שֶׁל כְּאֵב
וְזוֹ שֶׁמַּרְטִיבָה שְׂפָתָיו
הַחֲרוּכוֹת

Let Your Voice Be Heard, O Morning Blessings

A troubling thought
held my spirit in its palm
all night long
and I couldn't sleep—
its fingernails tore the images
of my dreams
and I drowned in the space
between the pits
and the world.

Like a soul mate that the heart
has despaired of ever seeing again
in the lands of the living,
the morning appeared.
Welcome, welcome,
angel of redemption!
And how the sick wait for the sunrise
as they turn from one side of pain
to the other,
and she, too, who moistens
the patient's scorched lips

בַּחֹשֶׁךְ
וְלִבָּהּ מָלֵא חֲרָדָה.

וְהִנֵּה הַשֶּׁמֶשׁ קַיֶּמֶת
פֹּה פֹּה –
וְקַיָּם עוֹלָם.
כְּבָר בָּתִּים מְסֻמָּנִים בְּזָהָב.

הֲשָׁמַעְנָה קוֹלְכֶן
בִּרְכוֹת הַשַּׁחַר הָאֲהוּבוֹת
בְּתוֹךְ הַנֹּגַהּ
הֲשָׁמַעְנָה קוֹלְכֶן הֶעָמֹק.
עוֹד מְעַט יֵהָפֵךְ הַנֹּגַהּ
לְאֵשׁ אוֹכֶלֶת
וְהַתִּקְוָה הַדַּקָּה תִּשָּׂרֵף.
אַךְ אוּלַי תַּעֲנֶה
הַנְּשָׁמָה
לְנַחֲמוּ נַחֲמוּ
שֶׁל רוּחוֹת הָעֶרֶב.

in the dark,
her heart filled with fear.

And see, the sun exists—
here, here—
and a world
exists.
The houses are already marked
with gold.

Let your voice be heard,
beloved blessings of the dawn,
in the midst of the radiance
let your deep voice be heard.
Soon the radiance will turn
into a devouring fire
and thin hope will be consumed.
But perhaps the soul will respond
to the *Comfort ye, comfort ye*
of the evening winds.

ציפור אחוזת קסם

כַּאֲשֶׁר הַגּוּף הָרַךְ
מָט לִנְפֹּל
וְהוּא מְגַלֶּה חֶרְדָּתוֹ מִפְּנֵי הַקֵּץ
לַנְּשָׁמָה,
מַצְמִיחַ עֵץ הַשִּׁגְרָה הַנָּמוּךְ
שֶׁאָבָק אֲכָלוֹ
עָלִים יְרֻקִּים פִּתְאֹם.
כִּי מֵרֵיחַ הָאַיִן יַפְרִיחַ
הָדוּר נָאֶה
וּבְצַמַּרְתּוֹ צִפּוֹר
אֲחוּזַת קֶסֶם.

Enchanted Bird

When the feeble body
is about to fall
and reveals its fear of death
to the soul,
the lowly tree of routine,
devoured by dust,
suddenly sprouts green leaves.
For out of the scent of Nothingness
the tree blossoms—
glorious, beautiful.
And in its crown—
an enchanted bird.

אשה שהגיעה לזקנה מופלגת

אִשָּׁה שֶׁהִגִּיעָה לְזִקְנָה מֻפְלֶגֶת
וְלֹא נוֹתַר בָּהּ שָׂרִיד מִטֵּרוּף הָאֵשׁ
מֵעֲסִיס הַקַּיִץ.
בְּשָׂרָהּ הַדַּק הָפַךְ לַאֲוִיר
וּמַבְהִיק בַּחֹשֶׁךְ כְּמָשָׁל עַתִּיק –
מְעוֹרֵר סְלִידָה בַּאֲנָשִׁים מְגֻשָּׁמִים
וּבְעָלִים יְרֻקִּים שֶׁל עֵץ הַתּוּת.

A Woman Who Has Reached a Very Old Age

A woman who has reached a very old age
with no trace left in her of the fire's madness,
the summer's juice—
Her thin flesh has turned into air
and gleams in the dark like an ancient fable,
repellent to green leaves of the mulberry tree
and to people still belonging to the earth.

לכל איש יש שם

לְכָל אִישׁ יֵשׁ שֵׁם
שֶׁנָּתַן לוֹ אֱלֹהִים
וְנָתְנוּ לוֹ אָבִיו וְאִמּוֹ
לְכָל אִישׁ יֵשׁ שֵׁם
שֶׁנָּתְנוּ לוֹ קוֹמָתוֹ וְאֹפֶן חִיּוּכוֹ
וְנָתַן לוֹ הָאָרִיג
לְכָל אִישׁ יֵשׁ שֵׁם
שֶׁנָּתְנוּ לוֹ הֶהָרִים
וְנָתְנוּ לוֹ כְּתָלָיו
לְכָל אִישׁ יֵשׁ שֵׁם
שֶׁנָּתְנוּ לוֹ הַמַּזָּלוֹת
וְנָתְנוּ לוֹ שְׁכֵנָיו
לְכָל אִישׁ יֵשׁ שֵׁם
שֶׁנָּתְנוּ לוֹ חֲטָאָיו
וְנָתְנָה לוֹ כְּמִיהָתוֹ
לְכָל אִישׁ יֵשׁ שֵׁם
שֶׁנָּתְנוּ לוֹ שׂוֹנְאָיו
וְנָתְנָה לוֹ אַהֲבָתוֹ

Each of Us Has a Name

Each of us has a name
given by God
and given by our parents

Each of us has a name
given by our stature and our smile
and given by what we wear

Each of us has a name
given by the mountains
and given by our walls

Each of us has a name
given by the stars
and given by our neighbors

Each of us has a name
given by our sins
and given by our longing

Each of us has a name
given by our enemies
and given by our love

לְכָל אִישׁ יֵשׁ שֵׁם
שֶׁנָּתְנוּ לוֹ חַגָּיו
וְנָתְנָה לוֹ מְלַאכְתּוֹ
לְכָל אִישׁ יֵשׁ שֵׁם
שֶׁנָּתְנוּ לוֹ תְּקוּפוֹת הַשָּׁנָה
וְנָתַן לוֹ עִוְרוֹנוֹ
לְכָל אִישׁ יֵשׁ שֵׁם
שֶׁנָּתַן לוֹ הַיָּם
וְנָתַן לוֹ
מוֹתוֹ.

Each of us has a name
given by our celebrations
and given by our work

Each of us has a name
given by the seasons
and given by our blindness

Each of us has a name
given by the sea
and given by
our death.

כל הלילה בכיתי

כָּל הַלַּיְלָה בָּכִיתִי
רִבּוֹנוֹ שֶׁל עוֹלָם
אוּלַי יֵשׁ מָוֶת שֶׁאֵין בּוֹ
אַלִּימוּת
מָוֶת שֶׁדּוֹמֶה לְפֶרַח.
כָּל הַלַּיְלָה הִפַּלְתִּי תַּחֲנוּנִי
אֲפִלּוּ אֲנִי עָפָר
תִּהְיֶה בִּי מְנוּחָה
לְהַבִּיט אֶל גָּבְהֵי שָׁמַיִם
עוֹד וְעוֹד וְעוֹד
לְהִפָּרֵד מִיָּפְיָם,

כָּל הַלַּיְלָה חָשַׁבְתִּי
בְּרִיּוֹת רַבּוֹת גָּרוֹת
בְּחָזִי הַכּוֹאֵב
וְסִפּוּרִים שׁוֹנִים,
צָרִיךְ לְהַדְלִיק נֵר
וּלְהַבִּיט עֲלֵיהֶם
בְּטֶרֶם אִישַׁן הַמָּוֶת.

All Night I Wept

All night I wept—
Sovereign of the universe,
perhaps there is death
without violence,
death that resembles a flower.

All night I implored—
Though I am dust,
let there be rest within me
that I may gaze toward heaven's heights
more and more
to separate from their beauty. *a seperation from
the conventional*

All night I thought—
Inside my aching chest
are many creatures
and all kinds of stories.
I must light a candle
and gaze upon them
before entering the sleep of death.

*only she has
the power to
share whats
inside her*

מקום של אש

אֲוִיר הָרִים אֲוִיר חַי
אָהוּב נוֹשֵׁב
בַּקֵּשׁ לְמַעֲנֵנוּ רַחֲמִים
מִן הָעֶלְיוֹן עַל כֹּל.
מָקוֹם שֶׁל אֵשׁ,
מָקוֹם שֶׁל בֶּכִי,
מָקוֹם שֶׁל טֵרוּף –
גַּם חָתָן וְכַלָּה
רַחֲמֵי שָׁמַיִם מְבַקְשִׁים
שֶׁלֹא יִתְפּוֹרֵר הָאֹפֶק.
כְּלָבִים וַחֲתוּלִים נִבְהָלִים.
רַק בַּצְּמָחִים לֹא נִדְלָחִים
עֲסִיסִים
פְּסִיעָה מִן הַתְּהוֹם,
רַק בַּפְּרָחִים הַמַּתִּיקוּת לֹא נְסוֹגָה
פְּסִיעָה מִן הַמָּוֶת.
כִּי הַצְּמָחִים עִם אַחֵר
מֵאִתָּנוּ,
חוּץ מֵעֲצֵי הַזַּיִת
שֶׁהֵם עֲצוּבִים וַחֲכָמִים כַּאֲנָשִׁים.
וְכַאֲשֶׁר מֶלֶךְ זָר וְאוֹיֵב
מַכְפִּישׁ שֶׁיָּכוֹתֵנוּ לָעִיר
שֶׁנָּבִיא אוֹהֵב
תָּלָה עַל צַוָּארָהּ

Place of Fire

Mountain air, living air,
breathing lover—
beg mercy for us
from the Supreme One.
Place of fire,
place of weeping,
place of madness—
even bride and groom
beg heaven's mercy
lest the horizon crumble.
Dogs and cats are alarmed.
Only in the plants
are the nectars not sullied
a step away from the abyss.
Only in the flowers
does the sweetness not retreat
a step away from death.
For the plants are a different nation
from us—
except for the olive trees,
which are sad and wise, like people.
And when a foreign, enemy king
tramples our ties to the city
upon whose neck
a loving prophet hung

סַפִּירִים נֹפֶךְ וְכַדְכֹּד –
נִרְעָדוֹת כְּמוֹ לִבִּי צַמְּרוֹת הַכֶּסֶף,
וְכַאֲשֶׁר מֶלֶךְ זָר וְאוֹיֵב
מַכְפִּישׁ אַהֲבָתֵנוּ הַנּוֹרָאָה
לְעִיר דָּוִד –
שׁוֹמְעִים הַשָּׁרָשִׁים
שֶׁל עֵץ הַזַּיִת אֵיךְ לוֹחֵשׁ דָּמוֹ
שֶׁל הַחַיָּל הַקָּטָן
בְּתוֹךְ הֶעָפָר:
הָעִיר רוֹבֶצֶת עַל חַיָּי.

sapphires, turquoise, and rubies,
the silver treetops tremble like my heart.
And when a foreign, enemy king
crushes our awesome love
for the City of David,
the roots of the olive tree
hear the small soldier's blood
whispering in the earth:
"The city is crouching on my life."

IV

ᐁᑲ ᑖᐧᐧᒡ ᐎᓇ ᑖᐧᐧᒡ

Surely a Mountain, Surely Fire

1977

אֵינֶנִּי אוֹהֶבֶת אֶת כָּל הָעֵצִים
שָׁוֶה –
נַפְשִׁי מְיַדֶּדֶת עִם עֵץ אַגָּס
חוֹלֶה.
הַכֹּל נָע מְשַׁנֶּה אֶת מְקוֹמוֹ
אֲנִי וְהוּא נְטוּעִים
בֶּחָצֵר שֶׁתְּקוּעָה בְּחָלָל
וְתַחְתֶּיהָ בּוֹר חָשׁוּךְ.
(בִּתּוֹ הַמְעֻנָּה שֶׁל דָּוִד הַמֶּלֶךְ
רוֹצָה בְּתוֹכוֹ לָמוּת
לַיְלָה לַיְלָה
כִּי אַלְפֵי שָׁנִים אֵינָן חַיִץ
לְחֶרְפָּתָהּ.)
כֵּן זוֹ אוֹתָהּ הֶחָצֵר
אַךְ בְּלִי הַפָּנִים אֲשֶׁר אָהַבְתִּי.
בְּאוֹתָהּ חָצֵר אֶעֱמֹד מוּל עֵץ
שֶׁקָּרֵב קִצּוֹ
נָפְלָה עֲטֶרֶת רַעֲנַנּוּתוֹ
וּפֵרוֹת שֶׁלּוֹ אֲשֶׁר הָיוּ מְתוּקִים
הָיוּ בְּשָׂמִים,
וְעָשׂוּ אֶת הַנֶּפֶשׁ
עַלִּיזָה וּבַת חוֹרִין,
הֵם כְּמוֹ מְעָרוֹת חוּמוֹת
מְלֵאוֹת נְחָשִׁים קְטַנִּים.
אַךְ כָּל הַצַּעַר הַזֶּה
הוּא שֶׁל לֵילוֹת שְׁקֵטִים.

152

*

I do not like all trees equally—
my soul befriends a pear tree
that is sick.
Everything moves, changes place;
I and it are planted
in a courtyard fixed in space
above a dark pit.
(Night after night,
King David's violated daughter
yearns to die here,
because millennia are no barrier
to her shame.)
Yes, this is the very courtyard
but without the face I loved.
In this yard, I stand
before a tree whose end is near—
the crown of its freshness has fallen,
and its once sweet, once fragrant fruits,
which delighted and freed the soul,
are like brown caves,
swarming with tiny snakes.

But all this sorrow
belongs to quiet nights.

בְּיוֹם אַף ה'
אֵינֶנִּי מְבַקֶּשֶׁת עָלָיו רַחֲמִים
אֵינֶנִּי מְבַקֶּשֶׁת עָלָיו
כִּי נַפְשִׁי מְסֻלֶּקֶת מִן הַצְּמָחִים.
וַהֲלֹא יִסְּרַנִי כָּל כָּךְ
עֵץ אֲפַרְסֵק קָטֹן
שֶׁגִּדַּלְתִּי בִּדְלִי,
כַּאֲשֶׁר נִרְמַס
עַל סַף לֵיל דִּין.

On the day of God's wrath,
I don't beg mercy for the tree,
I do not beg for it,
for my soul is removed from the plants.

And yet, how I suffered
when a small peach tree
that I raised in a bucket
was trampled
on the eve of Judgment Day.

עֶרֶב יוֹם הכיפורים

בְּעֶרֶב יוֹם הַכִּפּוּרִים
הִפְלַגְנוּ
מִנִּסְיוֹנוֹת שֶׁתַּמּוּ אֶל נִסְיוֹנוֹת שֶׁהֵחֵלּוּ.
עֶרֶב יוֹם הַכִּפּוּרִים הָיָה לָנוּ
רֵאשִׁית הַזְּמַן
בְּדִמְמַת אִי שֶׁהֵאִיר
יָם
בְּנֵרוֹת
שָׁם אֲמַצְתָּ אוֹתִי אֶל לִבְּךָ הַדּוֹאֵב
לִפְנֵי הַכֹּל יָכוֹל
בְּטֶרֶם תֵּלֵךְ לְהִתְפַּלֵּל עִם כֻּלָּם
בְּטֶרֶם תִּהְיֶה אֶחָד מִן הָעֵדָה
בַּהֵיכָל
אֶחָד מִן הָעֵצִים
בַּיַּעַר.

Yom Kippur Eve

On the eve of Yom Kippur,
we sailed
from experiences ended to experiences begun.
The eve of Yom Kippur was for us
the beginning of time
in the silence of an island
whose candles lit the sea.
There you held me to your sorrowing heart
in the presence of the Almighty,
before you went to pray with all the rest,
before you became one of the flock
in the chapel,
one of the trees
in the forest.

כַּאֲשֶׁר סְלָעִים מִתְפּוֹרְרִים
הָרוּחַ נוֹשֵׂאת מֵאוֹת קִילוֹמֶטְרִים מֶלַח
אֵלֶּה נוֹרְאוֹתָיו שֶׁל הַבּוֹרֵא.
אַךְ צִפּוֹר אַחַת מִתְעַקֶּשֶׁת לָשִׁיר
בּוֹאוּ קוֹלוֹת צִפֳּרִים
נִקְרוּ בְּנַפְשִׁי
הָעִירוּ אוֹתָהּ מִקִּפָּאוֹנָהּ
הוֹצִיאוּ אוֹתִי מִיָּם הַקֶּרַח

*

When boulders crumble,
the wind sweeps away miles of salt—
these are the awesome acts
of the Creator.
But one bird insists on singing.
Come, voices of birds,
peck at my soul,
awaken it from its freeze,
free me from the sea of ice.

✴

צֵל הָהָר הַלָּבָן
כִּסָּה אֶת פָּנַי וְיָדַי
וְדִמִּיתִי שֶׁנַּפְשִׁי חָפְשִׁית
כַּמֵּת.
צֵל עָצוּב כִּסָּה אֶת הַבַּיִת
וְאֶת עֲלֵי הַגֶּפֶן
אַךְ כַּאֲשֶׁר
בְּאֶרֶץ זָרָה
שֶׁהִיא רְחוֹבִי
נִגֵּן כִּנּוֹר
יָצָאתִי אֶל מִשׂוֹשׂ חָתָן וְכַלָּה
וְרָאִיתִי
כִּי הֵם שׁוֹזְרִים
תִּקְוָה עֲדִינָה עַד מְאֹד
וְרָאִיתִי
כִּי הֵמָּה שׁוֹזְרִים
תִּקְוָה אֲמִתִּית,
וְכָךְ בִּקַּשְׁתִּי בַּחֲשַׁאי:
יוֹצֵר הָאָדָם –
שֶׁלֹּא יִסְתָּעֲרוּ שֵׁדִים וּמַזִּיקִים
עַל דִּמְיוֹנָם
שֶׁיִּהְיֶה בִּנְיָנָם
בִּנְיַן עֲדֵי־עַד.

*

The shadow of the white mountain
covered my face and hands,
and I pictured my soul as free
as a dead man's.
A sad shadow draped the house
and the leaves of the grapevine.

But when, in the strange land
of my street,
a violin played,
I went out to see the joy
of a bride and groom.
And I saw them weaving
a delicate hope,
I saw them weaving
a true hope,
and in secret I prayed:

"Creator of humanity,
let no devils and evildoers
overtake their imaginings,
let their building
be everlasting."

תְּפִלָּתִי הַצְּמִיחָה
עָלִים יְרֻקִּים.
יָשַׁבְתִּי בְּצֵל הַקִּיקָיוֹן
וְלֹא יָדַעְתִּי עוֹד
מַה שֵׁם הַתַּחֲנָה
שֶׁהִגִּיעוּ אֵלֶיהָ חַיַּי.

My prayer
sprouted green leaves.
I sat in the shade of the gourd tree
and no longer knew
the name of the station
where my life had arrived.

מפיבושת

עֵינֶיךָ הַמְרַצְּדוֹת
צִפֳּרִים קְטַנּוֹת יוֹנְקוֹת דְּבַשׁ.

כַּאֲשֶׁר בָּכִיתָ
הַמֶּלֶךְ לֹא שָׁמַע.

כַּאֲשֶׁר נָפַלְתָּ
הָעוֹלָם לֹא חָזַר לְתֹהוּ וָבֹהוּ.

מְפִיבֹשֶׁת, חָלַמְתָּ
עַל יְדִידוּת תְּמִימָה יוֹתֵר.

מָאַסְתָּ בְּחָכְמַת הַנָּחָשׁ הַקַּדְמוֹנִי,
בְּנוֹ שֶׁל יְהוֹנָתָן.

Mephiboshet

Your flitting eyes—
small birds sipping nectar.

When you wept,
the king did not hear.

When you fell,
the world did not revert
to void-and-chaos.

Mephiboshet, you dreamt
of a more innocent friendship.

You abhorred the wisdom
of the ancient serpent,

O son of Jonathan.

כלימה רחוקה

אֲנִי אֲסִירַת תּוֹדָה לְעָלֶה יְרַקְרַק –
כִּי עָלֶה הוּא
יָד
שֶׁמּוֹשֶׁכֶת נַפְשִׁי מִן הַתְּהוֹם
בְּחִבָּה פְּשׁוּטָה מְשִׁיִּית
בְּלִי פְּסַק־דִּין עַל חַיַּי,
כִּי עָלֶה הוּא סִפּוּר מַדְהִים
שֶׁל רַעֲנַנּוּת שֶׁל תְּחִיַּת הַמֵּתִים.
אַךְ חֶלְקִי עִם אָדָם
וְלִפְנֵי אָדָם עִם יֵצֶר הַבְּגִידָה
שֶׁבּוֹ
אֶפְתַּח מַמְּגוּרוֹת רִשְׁמֵי
אֶחְשֹׂף כְּאֵבִי.

לְתוּגַת הַצִּיצִים הַנּוֹבְלִים
וּלְעַצְבוּת שֶׁל חַיְתוֹ אֶרֶץ
עוֹנִים רַק חוּשִׁי,
נַפְשִׁי עוֹמֶדֶת עַל כּוֹכָב אַחֵר
הִיא עוֹנָה לְאֵימָה שֶׁל יְלוּד־אִשָּׁה,
לִכְלִמָּה רְחוֹקָה.
עַל כֵּן עֶלְבּוֹנוֹ שֶׁל מְפִיבֹשֶׁת
מַרְעִיל אֶת קְרָבַי

166

Distant Shame

I am bound in gratitude
to a pale green leaf—
for a leaf
is a hand
that pulls my soul from the abyss
with a simple, silky affection,
with no judgment about my life;
for a leaf is a startling story of freshness
and revival of the dead.
But my lot remains with people—
and in the presence of people
with their inclination to betray
I open up the storehouse of my mind
and expose my pain.

To the sadness of wilting buds
and the sorrow of beasts
only my senses respond.
My soul stands on another planet
and responds to human terror
and distant shame.
And so the insult to Mephiboshet
poisons me within.

וְכַאֲשֶׁר הוּא נִכְנַס

בְּעֶרֶב שַׁבָּת בַּדִּמְדּוּמִים
בְּחִיּוּךְ נָבוֹךְ
וְעֵינַיִם תּוֹעוֹת,
אָמַרְתִּי:
מְפִיבֹשֶׁת נְסִיכִי הַזָּרוּק,
הַמֶּלֶךְ טוֹעֶן
כִּ אֵין בָּנוּ זִיק שֶׁל הוּמוֹר
כִּי לֹא הֵבַנּוּ כַּוָּנָתוֹ.

And when he entered—

at dusk on Sabbath eve,
with an embarrassed smile
and faltering eyes,
I said,
"Mephiboshet, my discarded prince,
the king claims that we lack all humor,
that we did not understand his intent."

אורנים עתיקים

"ועצים מותר להרוג?"
אמר פתאום ילד קטן
שעיניו כמו מצויירות.

כַּאֲשֶׁר הִפְשִׁירוּ הַשְּׁלָגִים
יָצְאוּ מִן הַהֲרִיסוֹת גְּבָרִים קוֹדְרִים
לִגְדֹעַ אֲרָנִים עַתִּיקִים רַבֵּי כֹחַ
שֶׁעָנוּ לְרוּחוֹת הֶהָרִים.
עֲנָפִים גְּמִישִׁים רֻמְּסוּ עַד דַּק
בַּחֲצֵרוֹת –
עֲנָפִים שֶׁצִּיְּרוּ בְּחָלָל תְּנוּעוֹת קַלִּילוֹת
מִפְּנִימִיּוּת הַצְּמִיחָה.
אֶת הַצֵּל הַיְרַקְרַק הִשְׁלִיכוּ
לָאַשְׁפַּתּוֹת
בָּעֲטוּ בַּבֹּשֶׁם, בַּשֶּׁרֶף.

Ancient Pines

"And trees—you're allowed to kill trees?"
blurted a small boy, whose eyes
were like something from a painting.

When the snows melted,
grim men emerged from the ruins
to fell ancient, powerful pines
that once responded to the mountain winds.
Limber branches were crushed to dust
in the courtyards,
branches that had sketched in space gentle motions
from the innermost flowering.
They tossed the pale green shadow
into the trash,
and kicked at the fragrance, the sap.

וָאִיקַץ וְהִנֵּה הַבַּיִת מוּאָר
אַךְ אֵין אִישׁ אִתִּי בַּבַּיִת –
וְעֶצֶב כָּזֶה
וְצַעַר.
וַהֲלֹא שִׂמְחַת הַשֶּׁמֶשׁ
דְּבַר יוֹם בְּיוֹמוֹ
וַהֲלֹא הַר
וַהֲלֹא אֵשׁ.
הוֹי
הַיֹּפִי נִתְקַע כְּמוֹ סַכִּין
בַּלֵּב.

*

I awoke— the house was lit,
but no one was there with me—
And what sadness
and pain—
Yet surely the joy of the sun
is an everyday matter,
and surely a mountain,
and surely fire—
Oh, beauty sticks like a knife
in the heart.

הַכֹּל הִשְׁתַּבֵּשׁ
מִפְּנֵי שֶׁלָּעַצְבוּת
הָיָה פִּתְאֹם
טַעַם לְוַאי שֶׁל בּוּשָׁה,
שֶׁל נְמִיכוּת־הָרוּחַ
בִּפְנֵי בָּשָׂר וָדָם.
לֹא,
אֵינֶנִּי יוֹדַעַת
אִם הַבְּרוֹשִׁים בֶּחָצֵר הַחֲדָשָׁה
יִהְיוּ טוֹבִים אֵלַי
אִם הַבְּרוֹשִׁים
שָׁמוּל הַגְּזוּזְטְרָה
יִהְיוּ יְדִידַי
כְּמוֹ שֶׁהָיָה
עֵץ הָאַגָּס הַמִּתְפַּלֵּעַ,
וְהָאֵלָה מַכְנִיסַת הָאוֹרְחִים
שֶׁנָּתְנָה אֶת פִּרְיָהּ
בְּעִקָּר לַיּוֹנִים
אַךְ גַּם לְצִפֳּרִים פִּתְאֹמִיּוֹת.

*

Everything went awry
for sadness suddenly
had an aftertaste of shame,
a meekness of spirit
in the face of flesh and blood.
No, I do not know
if the cypresses in the new yard
will be good to me,
if the cypresses opposite the balcony
will be my friends—
like the wormy pear tree
and the hospitable terebinth
that gave its fruit mostly to pigeons
but also to sudden birds.

בַּבֹּקֶר הִרְהַרְתִּי:
לֹא יָשׁוּב עוֹד קֶסֶם הַחַיִּים
לֹא יָשׁוּב.
פִּתְאֹם בְּבֵיתִי הַשֶּׁמֶשׁ
יֵשׁוּת חַיָּה לִי
וְהַשֻּׁלְחָן אֲשֶׁר עָלָיו לֶחֶם
זָהָב
וְהַפֶּרַח אֲשֶׁר עַל הַשֻּׁלְחָן וְהַסְּפָלִים
זָהָב
וּמֶה הָיָה לָעֶצֶב
גַּם בָּעֶצֶב נֹגַהּ.

*

In the morning, I thought:
"Life's magic will never return,
it won't return."
Suddenly in my house, the sun
is a living thing,
and the table with its bread—
gold.
And the flower and the cups—
gold.
And the sadness?
Even there—
radiance.

V

ה‫שוני המרהיב‬

The Spectacular Difference

1981

בחלומי

טִיַּלְנוּ בְּעִיר לֵילִית
וְחוֹגֶגֶת
פְּאֵר אַפְלוּלִי הָיָה סְבִיבֵנוּ
וְקָהָל שׁוֹקֵק.
לִבִּי הָיָה רַךְ עָלַי וְרַעֲנָן
כְּעֵץ שָׁתוּל עַל פַּלְגֵי מַיִם.

אוּלַי יְקִיצָה אֵינֶנָּה הַמַּמָּשׁ,
כִּי אֵיךְ אָבִין
שֶׁהַהוֹלֵךְ לְצִדִּי גָּבֹהַּ וְיָפֶה
רָחוֹק מִן הַיָּרֵחַ –
וְנִשְׁמָתוֹ לְפָנֶיךָ, יָהּ.

In My Dream

We strolled through a festive,
nocturnal city,
surrounded by dark splendor
and a bustling crowd.
My heart was tender and fresh
as a tree planted beside streams of water.

Perhaps waking is not what is real.
For how shall I understand
that the one walking by my side,
tall and beautiful,
far from the moon,
has his soul before You, God?

ידידות היסמין הלבן

לז'נט ולרובי

הַיַּסְמִין הַלָּבָן שֶׁעָשָׂה עָנָף בַּעֲצִיצִי
בְּהָדָר כָּזֶה
שָׁלוֹם סְבִיבוֹת יָפְיוֹ

בְּכַף הַיָּד שֶׁל נִיחוֹחוֹ
מְנַמְנֶמֶת נַפְשִׁי
חוֹלֶמֶת עַל מַעְיָן.

182

The Friendship of the White Jasmine

For Janet and Robbie

The white jasmine that put forth
a branch in my flowerpot
so gloriously,
peace surrounding its beauty—

In the palm of its fragrance,
my soul drifts in sleep,
dreaming of a fountain.

עֲנַף שֶׁל יַסְמִין

הַיֹּפִי נִתֵּק אֶת עַצְמוֹ
מִן הַיְסוֹד הַנּוֹבֵל שֶׁבַּצֶּמַח
הוּא נִמְלַט מִן הַגְּזֵרָה
וְלֹא שָׁב לֶעָפָר
עִם עָלִים מִתְפַּזְּרִים וְכָלִים,

אַט אַט נֶהְפַּךְ לְמַלְאָךְ
וְשָׁכַח אֶת בְּכִי הַתִּמּוֹרוֹת.

Jasmine Branch

Beauty detached itself
from the wilting of the plant,
fled from the decree
and did not return to dust
with the scattering, vanishing leaves.

Slowly it turned into an angel,
and forgot the wails of change.

*

מִן הָאַגָּדוֹת שֶׁנִּקְבְּרוּ
תַּחַת הֲרִיסוֹת חַגַּי
יָכֹלְתִּי לִבְנוֹת עִיר אֲהוּבָה
וְאֵיזֶה חֳרָשׁוֹת
וְאֵיזֶה בֻּסְתָּנִים...

*

From the legends buried
beneath the ruins of my celebrations,
I could have built a beloved city—
and what woods—
and what orchards—

הָאוֹר הַדַּק שֶׁל שְׁלוֹמִי

פִּרְפֵּר יָמָיו בְּגַן־עֵדֶן
דָּבַק בַּפֶּרַח שֶׁזָּרַעְתִּי
בַּסְּתָו
אוֹתִיּוֹת שֶׁל מַעְלָה בִּכְנָפָיו הַכְּתֻמּוֹת
סִימָנִים שֶׁל יָהּ.

בַּסִּימָנִים הָאֵלֶּה
שֶׁנֶּגֶד עֵינַי טָבְעוּ בֶּחָלָל
רִפְרֵף הָאוֹר הַדַּק
שֶׁל שְׁלוֹמִי.

The Fine Light of My Peace

The butterfly from the flower's
days in paradise—
the flower that I planted in the fall—
still clung, with heavenly letters
in its orange wings,
signs of God.

message in wings

In these signs
that drowned in space before my eyes,
the fine light of my peace
fluttered.

הפרפר הכתום

כַּאֲשֶׁר הַפַּרְפַּר הַכָּתֹם מְפַלֵּס דַּרְכּוֹ
בִּנְהַר שֶׁל צְבָעִים וְרֵיחוֹת
אֶל פֶּרַח בֶּן דְּמוּתוֹ וְדָבֵק בּוֹ
כְּמוֹ הָיָה פֶּרַח זֶה
כּוֹכָב הָאֲנִי הַסּוֹדִי שֶׁלּוֹ
מִתְעוֹרֶרֶת תִּקְוָה סוֹאֶנֶת וְחֶסְרַת פֵּשֶׁר
בְּכָל הַלְּבָבוֹת.

וְכַאֲשֶׁר נוֹטֵשׁ אוֹתוֹ מְרַחֵף יָפֶה
אֶת עֲלֵי הַכּוֹתֶרֶת שֶׁעָיְפוּ
וְנֶעֱלָם בֶּחָלָל
מֵקִיץ בַּתֵּבֵל הָרֶגַע הַגַּלְמוּד,
נֶעֱלֶמֶת נְשָׁמָה בָּאֵין־סוֹף.

The Orange Butterfly

When the orange butterfly wends its way
through a river of colors and scents
toward its flower-mate, and clings
as though this flower were the star
of its secret self—
an inexplicable clamor of hope
rises in every heart.

we search so long
to see & know
ourselves... we
hold on

↓

And when that beautiful flutterer
abandons the weary petals
and vanishes in space,
the lonely moment wakens in the world,
a soul vanishes in infinity.

beyond human/
freedom

191

הַגֶּשֶׁם הָרִאשׁוֹן
אַלְפֵי רְבָבָה רַעֲנַנּוּת
בְּלִי אוֹת שֶׁל קַיִן.
וְהַדְּוַי לֹא יִלְחַשׁ עוֹד
לְנַפְשִׁי
אֲנִי הַמֶּלֶךְ
לֹא יַגִּיד עוֹד
אֲנִי הַשַּׁלִּיט.
כָּל טִפָּה וְטִפָּה
הִיא זָקָה
בֵּינִי וּבֵין הַדְּבָרִים
זָקָה
בֵּינִי וּבֵין הָעוֹלָם.
וְכַאֲשֶׁר הַלַּיְלָה
מַעֲלֶה אֶת הַתְּהוֹם
הַתְּהוֹם מַעֲלֶה
שָׂדוֹת וְגַנִּים.

*

The first rain—
a plenitude of freshness
with no sign of Cain.
And agony will no longer
whisper to my soul,
"I am the king."
No longer will it say,
"I am the ruler."
Each drop is a link
between me and things,
a link
between me and the world.
And when night
conjures up the abyss,
the abyss conjures up
fields and gardens.

לזכרה של זיוה לויצקי

שְׂעָרָהּ נְחֹשֶׁת קָלָל
נוֹצֵץ כְּאֶלֶף שְׂמָחוֹת
בַּשֶּׁמֶשׁ,
וְהִנֵּה קָרֵב אִישׁ
עִם דּוֹרוֹנוֹת וּשְׁבָחִים לְיָפְיָהּ.
עוֹד יֵסֵב
וְהַיְשִׁישָׁה לָחֲשָׁה:
בִּי לְבָתִּי
אַל תֵּצְאִי הַחוּצָה,
פֶּן יִקָּחֵךְ הַחֹשֶׁךְ
וְלֹא אֵדַע לְהַצִּילֵךְ מִיָּדוֹ,
פֶּן יִרְאֶה צַמָּתֵךְ
יָרֵחַ הוֹזֶה.
כֵּן, זֶה הָאִישׁ –
אַךְ יְשִׁישָׁה עֲיֵפַת־בְּכִי
זוֹעֶקֶת:
אַל תִּפְתְּחִי אֶת הַשַּׁעַר
כִּי לֹא אֵדַע
לְהַצִּילֵךְ מִיָּדוֹ שֶׁל הַיָּם.
לָמָּה לֹא לָחֲשָׁה:
הִנָּךְ בִּרְשׁוּת הַפְּרִיחָה
אַל תֵּעָנִי לַמָּוֶת
אַל תֵּעָנִי לַמָּוֶת –
וְלָמָּה אֲנַחְנוּ שָׁתַקְנוּ.

*

Her hair, burnished copper,
shining in the sun like a thousand joys—
and here a man approaches,
bearing gifts and praises of her beauty.
While he is still near,
an old woman whispers,
"Please, my darling girl, don't go out
lest the darkness take you
and I won't know how to save you
from its hand,
lest the delirious moon
see your braid."

Yes, this is the man—
but an old woman,
weary from weeping,
cries out, "Don't open the gate
for I won't know how to save you
from the hand of the sea."

Why did she not whisper,
"Here you are in the domain of flowering—
don't respond to death,
don't respond to death"?
And why did we keep silent?

ילדים בבית חינוך עוורים

קָלְעָנוּ זֵרִים בְּגִנַּת בֵּיתָם הַקּוֹדֵר
וְטַרְפֵּי שׁוֹשַׁנִּים רִחֲפוּ בָּאֲוִיר
נְעָרִים קְטַנִּים פָּלְשׁוּ לְשָׁם
חִוְרִים וְנִסְעָרִים
בְּרִכּוּז פְּרָאִי צָדוּ קוֹלוֹת
שֶׁמַּשְׁמִיעַ הַיְקוּם
מִשְׁשׁוּ פְּנֵי הָעוֹלָם.

נִיחוֹחַ הַשּׁוֹשַׁנִּים אָפַף אוֹתָם
אַךְ הֵם לֹא עָנוּ לַעֹנֶג הָרַךְ.
כִּי טָרְחוּ עַד אֵין קֵץ
לִמְצֹא אֶת הַשְּׁבִיל הַסּוֹדִי
שֶׁמּוֹבִיל לְלֵב לִבָּהּ שֶׁל הַשֶּׁמֶשׁ,
אֶת שְׁבִיל הַלֹּא רוֹאִים.

Children in the School for the Blind

We plaited wreaths in the garden
of their somber house
and rose petals fluttered in the air.
Small boys invaded,
stormy and pale,
with fierce concentration
stalking the sounds of the universe,
groping at the face of the world.

The scent of roses enveloped them
but they did not yield to the gentle pleasure.
Relentlessly, they worked
to find the secret path
that leads to the heart of the sun—
the path of the unsighted.

מי יעמוד בפני יופיו של האור

וָאֶשָּׂא אֶת רָגְזִי לְהַרְאוֹתוֹ לָאוֹר
לְבַקֵּשׁ נִחוּמִים מִיָּפְיוֹ
אַךְ לֹא הָיִיתִי טוֹבָה לְפָנָיו,
לֹא הָיִיתִי טוֹבָה לְפָנָיו.

"מַדּוּעַ חַיַּיִךְ כֵּהִים", אָמַר,
"הֲלֹא אֵינֵךְ בְּבוֹר־תַּחְתִּיּוֹת,
אֵין זֶה כִּי אִם חֹסֶר אַהֲבָה".
וָאֵבְךְּ
וָאֵבְךְּ הַרְבֵּה מְאֹד.

Who Can Resist the Beauty of the Light

I bore my anger to show to the light,
seeking comfort in its beauty,
but I was not worthy in its eyes,
I was not worthy in its eyes.

"Why is your life dark?" it said.
"You are not in the depths of the pit.
This must be a lack of love."

And I wept.
I wept deeply.

אורנים נדהמי שמש

אֳרָנִים נִדְהֲמֵי שֶׁמֶשׁ
הֵדִיפוּ נִיחוֹחַ פְּרָאִי –
אוֹתוֹ אוֹן מְהַמֵּם מִפְּנִימִיּוּת הַצְּמִיחָה
עָשָׂה אוֹתִי שׁוּב
בַּת־בַּיִת בָּעוֹלָם,
אַךְ אֶת הָעִקָּר לֹא הִגִּיד לִי;
מָה הַכַּוָּנָה הָאֱלֹהִית
בִּצְמָחִים צָצִים וְנוֹבְלִים.
גַּם תַּכְלִית חַיַּי
וְתַכְלִית מוֹתִי
לֹא אֵדַע בָּעוֹלָם הַזֶּה.

Sun-Startled Pines

Sun-startled pines
wafted a wild fragrance—
the same stunning strength
from the inmost flowering
made the world my home again
but did not reveal the core,
the divine intention
in budding and wilting plants.
And the point of my life
and the point of my death—
I will not know in this world.

עֵץ הַחַיִּים

הָאִישׁ הַצָּעִיר צָחַק
אַחַר כָּךְ סִפֵּר בְּעֵינַיִם מְאִירוֹת
וּבְשׂוֹם שֵׂכֶל
עַל תָּכְנִית הַדְּבַשׁ וְהַשֶּׁמֶן
וְעַל הַסַּכָּנוֹת.
פַּחַד לֹא עֲמָמוֹ,
גַּם אִשְׁתּוֹ וְעוֹלָלָיו נְסוּכֵי שֶׁמֶשׁ.
חִבָּתָם שָׁלְחָה אוֹתוֹת
אֶל יוֹמִי הַשּׁוֹקֵעַ.
מִשְׁפָּחָה זוֹ –
עֵץ הַחַיִּים בְּתוֹךְ הָעִיר הַמְסֻלַּעַת.

The Tree of Life

The young man laughed.
Later, with shining eyes
full of wisdom,
he told of the plan of honey and oil
and of the dangers.
Fear did not darken him.
His wife and offspring, too,
were bathed in sunlight.
Their affection sent forth signs
into my sinking day.
This family—
the tree of life in the rocky city.

הָיָה מַשֶּׁהוּ מַבְהִיל
בְּגוֹן הַשָּׁמַיִם
הִשְׁתּוֹמַמְתִּי שֶׁצַּמְּרוֹת הָעֵצִים
מִתְנַדְנְדוֹת בְּקַלִּילוּת
בְּלִי צֵל שֶׁל חֲרָדָה.
רָצִיתִי לִבְרֹחַ מִן הָרָקִיעַ הַלָּבָן
אַךְ הַגִּנָּה הַקְּטַנָּה
הֶרְאֲתָה לִי סִימָנִים
כִּי לֹא כָּלוּ רַחֲמָיו.

*

There was something startling
in the hue of the sky.
I was amazed that the treetops
swayed gently
with no shadow of fear.
I wanted to flee from the white sky
but the small garden showed me signs
that His mercy had not ceased.

שיר עתיק עד מאוד

שִׁיר עַתִּיק עַד מְאֹד
הֱקִיצַנִי לַחַיִּים
כַּאֲשֶׁר גֵּרֵשׁ
אֶת נְמִיכוּת הָרוּחַ מִקִּרְבִּי
בִּשְׂפָתֵי מְלָכִים.

שִׁיר דּוֹר שֶׁנָּדַם
לִפְנֵי עֵדֶן וְעֶדְנִים
הֱקִיצַנִי לַחַיִּים.

Ancient Song

A very ancient song
wakened me to life
when it banished humility from me
with the lips of kings.

A song of a generation
that went silent
ages and ages ago
awakened me to life.

ראש לא מסורק

מִלָּה אַחַת
נִפְּצָה אֶת כָּל הַפָּנָסִים
מִלָּה אַחַת הָפְכָה
רְחוֹב מוּאָר
לְיַעַר חָשׁוּד.
הַמַּלְאָךְ שֶׁנִּגְלָה אֶל הָגָר
בָּא אֶל הַיַּעַר הַנּוֹרָא
בָּא אֶל סוֹף הָעוֹלָם
לָגַעַת בְּיָדָהּ.
אַךְ הִיא נִמְלְטָה מִן הַמַּלְאָךְ
כְּמוֹ מִמְּקַסֵּם שָׁוְא
זוֹעֶקֶת:
אֵינְךָ קַיָּם אֵינְךָ קַיָּם אֵינְךָ קַיָּם
אַל תְּפַתֵּנִי בְּסוֹדוֹת שֶׁל רוּחַ.
מַעְיָן רָץ לִקְרָאתָהּ
בְּנִצְנוּצֵי מַיִם
עִם עֲנָפִים וְעָלִים,
אַךְ הִיא
רְטֻבָּה כֻּלָּהּ
בָּכְתָה:
אֲבוֹי לְנַפְשִׁי
שׁוּב תַּעְתּוּעִים.
אָחוֹת קְטַנָּה
רֹאשׁ לֹא מְסֹרָק
אַל תִּבְרְחִי מִצְּלִיל הַמַּלְאָכִים,

Uncombed Hair

A single word
shattered all the lights,
a single word
turned a lit street
into a dark forest.
The angel who revealed himself to Hagar
came to the terrible forest,
came to the end of the world
to touch her hand.
But she fled from the angel
as from a mirage,
crying,
"You don't exist, you don't exist,
you don't exist—
don't tempt me with empty secrets."

A fountain rushed toward her,
shimmering with water,
bearing branches and leaves,
but she, completely soaked, cried,
"My poor soul,
delusions again!"

Little sister with uncombed hair,
do not flee from the sound of angels.

חַיַּיִךְ מְצִיאוּת הוֹמָה
בְּשָׂרֵךְ אֵינֶנּוּ מָשָׁל,
וְהָאִישׁ הָאַדְמוֹנִי
יְדִיד הַשֶּׁמֶשׁ
יוֹדֵעַ שֶׁאַתְּ קַיִץ
יוֹדֵעַ שֶׁאַתְּ עֵץ פְּרִי.

Your life hums with yearning,
your flesh is not a fable,
and the red-haired man,
friend of the sun,
knows you are summer,
knows you are a fruit-bearing tree.

אִי

אֲנִי דוֹרֶכֶת עַל הָאֲדָמָה
כְּמוֹ עַל גּוּף חַי
כְּאוֹתָם פְּלִיטֵי אֳנִיָּה
שֶׁעָמְדוּ עַל גַּבּוֹ שֶׁל לִוְיָתָן
כִּי טָעוּ בְּמַרְאֵה הָעֵינַיִם.

אֲנִי דוֹרֶכֶת עַל הֶעָפָר
שֶׁתַּחְתָּיו מְדַבְּרִים הַמַּיִם
מְדַבְּרִים שָׁרָשִׁים
מְדַבְּרוֹת מַתָּכוֹת
קוֹל הֲמוֹנָם מַחֲרִישׁ אֶת אָזְנַי
מְסַחְרֵר אֶת לִבִּי
גַּם הָאֲוִיר מִתְנוֹעֵעַ וְשָׁר
וּבַגְּבָהִים מִתְפּוֹצְצִים עוֹלָמוֹת.

רַק הַמַּחֲשָׁבָה עַל אֱלֹהִים
הִיא אִי בַּמְּעַרְבֹּלֶת.

Island

I step on the earth
as on a living body—
like those who jumped ship
to stand on the back of a whale
because their eyes deceived them.

I step on the dust of the earth
beneath which the water speaks,
roots speak,
metals speak.
Their noise deafens my ears,
dizzies my heart.
The air, too, sways and sings,
and in the heights, worlds explode.

Only the thought of God
is an island in the whirl.

ברשות הירח

בְּנִשְׁמָתוֹ יֵשׁ עוֹד עִקְבוֹת הַשֶּׁמֶשׁ
יֵשׁ עוֹד הֵד מֵאוֹתָן תְּשׁוּאוֹת
אַךְ חִיּוּכוֹ וּתְנוּעוֹתָיו
כְּבָר בִּרְשׁוּת הַיָּרֵחַ
שֶׁמֵּאִיר אֶת הַשַּׁעַר
אֶל הָעוֹלָם הַכָּמוּס.

נִשְׁמָתוֹ יוֹדַעַת שֶׁכֻּלָּנוּ שָׁוִים
כְּלַפֵּי שָׁמַיִם
כֻּלָּנוּ עָפָר וָאֵפֶר
אַךְ אֵין בְּכֹחוֹ לִשְׁכֹּחַ
שֶׁהוּא אֶחָד מִצֶּאֱצָאֵי הַמֶּלֶךְ
וְזֶה שֶׁבָּז לוֹ
הָיָה מְשָׁרֵת עַל אוֹתוֹ כּוֹכָב.

In the Moon's Domain

In his soul are traces of the sun
and an echo of the old applause,
but his gestures and smile
are now in the moon's domain—
the moon, which lights the gate
to the hidden world.

His soul knows that we are all the same
in the eyes of heaven,
we are all of us dust and ashes.
But he cannot forget that he
is the descendant of the king
and the one who scorns him now
was a servant on the same planet.

בפרוזדור

בַּפְּרוֹזְדוֹר
אִשָּׁה אַחַת רָצְתָה לְהַגִּיד לָךְ
מַשֶּׁהוּ חָשׁוּב.
וַאֲנִי צָעַקְתִּי
אֵין דָּבָר חָשׁוּב
אֵין שׁוּם דָּבָר חָשׁוּב
כִּי יָמָיו סְפוּרִים.

In the Hallway

In the hallway
a woman wanted to tell you
something important.
And I cried out—
"There is nothing important,
nothing at all that's important,
for his days are numbered."

הלווייתנים

מַה הִפְחִיד כָּל כָּךְ אֶת הַלְּוְיְתָנִים
שֶׁנִּמְלְטוּ מִן הַיָּם
לָמוּת קְבוּצוֹת קְבוּצוֹת
– תַּחַת כִּפַּת הַשָּׁמַיִם
שֶׁבָּרְחוּ בִּבֶהָלָה
מִמַּעֲמַקֵּי אוֹקְיָנוֹס
לִגְוֹעַ עַל פְּנֵי שִׁמְמַת הַחוֹל.
לַשָּׁוְא מַדְעָנִים הֵאִירוּ בִּפְנָס
אֶת שִׁגְעוֹן פַּחְדָּם,
הַסּוֹד שֶׁגָּר בְּהָרֵי הַחֹשֶׁךְ
מַקְשִׁיב לְדִבְרֵיהֶם
וּמְחַיֵּךְ לְנַפְשׁוֹ.

The Whales

What was it that so frightened the whales
that they left the sea
to die in hordes
under the dome of the sky,
that they fled in panic
from the ocean's depths
to waste away on the desolate sand?
In vain the scientists shine their lights
on the madness of this fear.
The secret that dwells
in the mountains of darkness
hears their words
and smiles to itself.

שתיקה כבדה

הַמָּוֶת יִקַּח אֶת הַשֵּׁנִי הַמַּרְהִיב
שֶׁבֵּין אֵשׁ לְמַיִם
וְיַשְׁלִיכֵהוּ לַתְּהוֹם.

שְׁתִיקָה כְּבֵדָה כְּפַר
תִּרְבַּץ עַל הַשֵּׁמוֹת
שֶׁנָּתַן הָאָדָם לְעוֹפוֹת הַשָּׁמַיִם
וּלְחַיַּת הַשָּׂדֶה
לִשְׁמֵי הָעֶרֶב
לַמֶּרְחַקִּים הָעֲצוּמִים בֶּחָלָל
וְלִדְבָרִים סְמוּיִים מִן הָעַיִן.

שְׁתִיקָה כְּבֵדָה כְּפַר
תִּרְבַּץ עַל כָּל הַמִּלִּים.
וְקָשָׁה תִּהְיֶה עָלַי הַפְּרִידָה
מִשֵּׁמוֹת שֶׁל דְּבָרִים
כְּמוֹ מִן הַדְּבָרִים עַצְמָם.

יוֹדֵעַ תַּעֲלוּמוֹת
הֲבִינֵנִי מַה לְּבַקֵּשׁ בְּיוֹם אַחֲרוֹן.

Heavy Silence

Death will take the spectacular difference
between fire and water
and cast it to the abyss.

Heavy silence
will crouch like a bull
on the names we have given
the birds of the sky
and the beasts of the field,
the evening skies,
the vast distances in space,
and things hidden from the eye.

Heavy silence will crouch like a bull
on all the words.
And it will be as hard for me to part
from the names of things
as from the things themselves.

O Knower of Mysteries,
help me understand
what to ask for
on the final day.

VI

אתרמ לכ ינפלמ

Beyond All Distance

1984

באותו ליל כוכבים

בְּאוֹתוֹ לֵיל כּוֹכָבִים בִּקְשָׁה יַלְדוּתִי
אֶת בּוֹרֵא הָעוֹלָם.

הַשָּׁנִים שֶׁנִּגְּרוּ כַּמַּיִם,
שׁוּם עֶצֶב
וְשׁוּם אָדָם
לֹא יוּכְלוּ לְהַשְׁכִּיחַ מִמֶּנִּי
מֶרְחַקִּים
שֶׁנִּבְדְּלוּ מִכָּל מֶרְחָק.

On That Night of Stars

On that night of stars,
my childhood sought
the Creator of the world.

Years that spill like water,
sadness,
people—
none of these can make me forget
distances
beyond all distance.

הפוגה

למחבל שהציל שבוי ישראלי
מידי המחבלים
כאשר רצו לעשות בו שפטים

תְּנוּעַת יָד מְבַטֶּלֶת
אֶת הַהֲזָיוֹת עַל עֵנוּיִים,
תְּנוּעַת יָדוֹ
שֶׁל אֶחָד מִזְאֵבֵי הַהִתְאַבְּדוּת –
נַעַר שׁוֹקֵק
שֶׁבָּחַל פִּתְאֹם בַּשִּׂנְאָה
כִּי נַפְשׁוֹ גִּלְתָה לוֹ:
הַשִּׂנְאָה מְשַׁקֶּרֶת
הַשִּׂנְאָה מְשַׁקֶּרֶת
הַשִּׂנְאָה מְשַׁקֶּרֶת –
וְכֹחַ דִּמְיוֹנוֹ פָּרַץ
אֶל שְׁבִיל חָדָשׁ
עִם קוֹלוֹת הַיַּלְדוּת וְהַמּוֹפְתִים.
כַּאֲשֶׁר הֵקִיץ בּוֹ הַטּוֹב הַהְיוּלִי
הִצִּיל אֶת הַשָּׁבוּי
כַּאֲשֶׁר יָצָא נָהָר מֵעֵדֶן פְּנִימִיּוּתוֹ
נָתַן לוֹ מַיִם
לִחְיוֹתוֹ בַּמִּדְבָּר.
אַט אַט נָסוֹגָה לְאָחוֹר
מִפְלֶצֶת הַנְּקָמָה
וְנִגְלוּ עוֹלָמוֹת רַעֲנַנִּים שֶׁל תִּקְוָה

Pause

*For the terrorist who saved an Israeli prisoner
from the hands of the other terrorists
who wanted to torture him*

A gesture of the hand
wipes out the fantasies of torture—
a gesture
by one of the wolves of suicide,
an eager youth who suddenly
set hate aside
because his soul revealed to him:
Hatred lies,
hatred lies,
hatred lies.
And the force of his imaginings
burst upon a new path
with the sounds of childhood
and of miracles.
When the primordial good
awoke in him,
he saved the prisoner.
When a river flowed from his inner Eden,
he gave him water
to revive him in the desert.
Slowly the monster of vengeance
retreated,
and fresh worlds of hope

וְשִׂמְחַת מַעְיָנוֹת נִכְבְּדֵי־מַיִם.
אוֹיָהּ!

שְׁנֵיהֶם יָדְעוּ:
אֵין זוֹ כָּל הָאֱמֶת,
זוֹ הֲפוּגָה
בְּאִי יָרֹק,
הָאִי שֶׁהוּא מִחוּץ לְכָל לְאֹם
וּלְכָל מוֹצָא

בָּאִי הַזֶּה בְּאַחַת הַמְּעָרוֹת
פָּקַח אֶת עֵינָיו הַשָּׁלוֹם.

and the joy of wells rich with water
were revealed.

Oh! Both of them knew—
this was not the whole truth,
this was a pause
on a green island
beyond all nations,
beyond all origins.

On this island, in one of the caves,
peace opened its eyes.

*

לֹא אֲרַחֵף בֶּחָלָל
מִשֻׁלַּחַת רֶסֶן
פֶּן יִבְלַע עָנָן
אֶת הַפַּס הַדַּקִּיק שֶׁבְּלִבִּי
שֶׁמַּפְרִיד בֵּין טוֹב לְרָע.
אֵין לִי קִיּוּם
בְּלִי הַבְּרָקִים וְהַקּוֹלוֹת
שֶׁשָּׁמַעְתִּי בְּסִינַי.

*

I shall not float unreined
in space
lest a cloud swallow
the thin band in my heart
that separates good from evil.
I have no existence
without the lightning and thunder
that I heard at Sinai.

כאשר געגועים

כַּאֲשֶׁר גַּעְגּוּעִים פּוֹרְעִים
אֶת שְׂעָרָהּ הַבָּהִיר
הִיא לוֹחֶשֶׁת לָהֶם:
חִדְלוּ
הֱיִיתֶם עָלַי לְטֹרַח,
מְאֹרֶשֶׂת אֲנִי
לַנָּהָר לֵילִי
שֶׁנּוֹרָא מִן הַיָּם
הַנָּהָר שֶׁשְּׁמוֹ רַחֲמִים.

When Yearnings

When yearnings dishevel
her light hair,
she whispers to them,
"Stop.
You have burdened me.
I am betrothed
to a nocturnal river
more awesome than the sea,
the river called compassion."

שני יסודות

הַלֶּהָבָה אוֹמֶרֶת לַבְּרוֹשׁ
כַּאֲשֶׁר אֲנִי רוֹאָה
כַּמָּה אַתָּה שַׁאֲנָן
כַּמָּה עוֹטֶה גָאוֹן
מַשֶּׁהוּ בְּתוֹכִי מִשְׁתּוֹלֵל
אֵיךְ אֶפְשָׁר לַעֲבֹר אֶת הַחַיִּים
הַנּוֹרָאִים הָאֵלֶּה
בְּלִי שֶׁמֶץ שֶׁל טֵרוּף
בְּלִי שֶׁמֶץ רוּחָנִיּוּת
בְּלִי שֶׁמֶץ שֶׁל דִּמְיוֹן
בְּלִי שֶׁמֶץ שֶׁל חֵרוּת
בְּגַאֲוָה עַתִּיקָה וְקוֹדֶרֶת.
לוּ יָכֹלְתִּי הָיִיתִי שׂוֹרֶפֶת
אֶת הַמִּמְסָד
שֶׁשִּׂמוֹ תְּקוּפוֹת הַשָּׁנָה
וְאֶת הַתְּלוּת הָאֲרוּרָה שֶׁלְּךָ
בָּאֲדָמָה, בָּאֲוִיר, בַּשֶּׁמֶשׁ, בַּמָּטָר וּבַטַּל.
הַבְּרוֹשׁ שׁוֹתֵק,
הוּא יוֹדֵעַ שֶׁיֵּשׁ בּוֹ טֵרוּף
שֶׁיֵּשׁ בּוֹ חֵרוּת
שֶׁיֵּשׁ בּוֹ דִּמְיוֹן
שֶׁיֵּשׁ בּוֹ רוּחָנִיּוּת
אַךְ הַשַּׁלְהֶבֶת לֹא תָבִין
הַשַּׁלְהֶבֶת לֹא תַאֲמִין.

Two Elements

The flame says to the cypress:
"When I see how calm,
how full of pride you are,
something inside me goes wild—
How can one live this awesome life
without a touch of madness,
of spirit,
of imagination,
of freedom,
with only a grim, ancient pride?
If I could, I would burn down
the establishment
that we call the seasons,
along with your cursed dependence
on earth and air and sun,
on rain and dew."

The cypress does not answer.
He knows there is madness in him,
and freedom,
and imagination,
and spirit.
But the flame will not understand,
the flame will not believe.

על העובדות

לסולי כהן

נַפְשִׁי אוֹמֶרֶת:
הָעֻבְדּוֹת מַסְתִּירוֹת אֶת הַיָּם.
חוּשַׁי אוֹמְרִים:
הָעֻבְדּוֹת אִי בָּאוֹקְיָנוֹס.
נַפְשִׁי אוֹמֶרֶת:
הָעֻבְדּוֹת חוֹמָה סְבִיב הָאֲנִי.
חוּשַׁי אוֹמְרִים:
הָעֻבְדּוֹת חַלּוֹן מוּאָר בַּחֹשֶׁךְ
צֹהַר לִפְנִימִיּוּתִי.
וּמֵאָז וּמֵעוֹלָם אוֹמֶרֶת הַתְּהוֹם:
הָעֻבְדּוֹת אַרְיֵה
שׁוֹאֵג בֶּחָלָל
קַיָּם
קַיָּם
קַיָּם.

236

About Facts

For Solly Cohen

My soul says:
"Facts conceal the sea."

My senses say:
"Facts are an island in the ocean."

My soul says:
"Facts are a wall around the self."

My senses say:
"Facts are a window lit in the dark,
a lens into my core."

And from the beginning,
the abyss has said:
"Facts are a lion
roaring in space
existing
existing
existing."

בבית החולים

א. כי יימכר סוס בשוק

כִּי יִמָּכֵר סוּס בַּשּׁוּק
אִישׁ לֹא יִשְׁאַל אֶת הַנֶּפֶשׁ הַסּוּסִית
אִם מַרְשָׁה הִיא
לִפְתֹּחַ אֶת פִּי הַסּוּס בְּיָד זָרָה
וּבְאֵיבָרָיו לָגַעַת.
אֶת בְּשָׂרֵי הַנִּכְלָם הִנִּיחוּ
לִפְנֵי דְרָקוֹן הַמַּדָּע
בְּלִי לִשְׁאֹל אֶת נַפְשִׁי

עֲשָׂרָה רָאשִׁים שֶׁל דְּרָקוֹן נַעֲלֶה
הִתְבּוֹנְנוּ בְּעֶנְיִי
בְּלִי לִשְׁאֹל אֶת נַפְשִׁי

In the Hospital

1. When a horse is sold in the marketplace

When a horse is sold in the marketplace,
no one asks the horse-soul
if it will allow a strange hand
to open the horse's mouth,
to touch its limbs.
They set my shamed flesh
before the dragon of science
without asking my soul.

Ten heads of the lofty dragon
observed my misery
without asking my soul.

ב. מעבר לקיר ישישה חולה

בְּקוֹלָהּ הַמְרֻסָּק וְהַמְעֻנֶּה
אֵין הָרַעַל
שֶׁבִּנְהִי הַזְּרוּקָה,
אֲפִלּוּ בְּרֶגַע שֶׁל סְחִי שֶׁל שָׁאָט
בִּכְיָהּ
בְּכִי יַלְדָּה עֲלֵי-אִמָּהּ
בְּלִי חֲשָׁשׁ
מִקְּרִיצוֹת, מִסְּלִידָה, מִקֶּלֶס.
בְּעֶרֶב טָס אֵלַי מֵחֲדָרָהּ צְחוֹק דַּק דַּק
זִכָּרוֹן מְקֻיָּם אַחֵר.
וּפִתְאֹם נֶהֱמָה עֲרִירִית בַּחֹשֶׁךְ
נַהֲמַת פַּחְדָּהּ
מִן הַתְּנוּמָה וּמִן הַיְקִיצָה.

בַּשַּׁחַר
שׁוּב שָׁקְטָה הַזְּקֵנָה כִּפְרַח נוֹבֵל
וְחִיּוּךְ הָאָחוֹת
נֶחָמָה לָהּ.
יְשִׁישָׁה זוֹ לֹא נָטְשָׁה מִתּוֹךְ כַּעַס
אֶת הַדּוּ-שִׂיחַ עִם אֲנָשִׁים
וְעִם אֱלֹהִים.
אִמִּי הָיְתָה דוֹמָה לָהּ
בְּיַחֲסָהּ לַשָּׁמַיִם
בְּתוֹךְ גֵּיא צַלְמָוֶת.
אַךְ לְאִמִּי הָיוּ חֲשָׁשׁוֹת הַרְבֵּה.

2. Beyond the wall, a sick old woman

In her broken, tortured voice—
no poison,
no wail of abandonment.
Even in a moment of filth, of revulsion,
she weeps
the way a child weeps for mama,
without fear of mockery or scorn.
In the evening, a thin laugh
flies toward me from her room—
a memory of another existence.
And suddenly a lonely growl in the dark—
her terror of sleeping
and of waking.

At dawn, once again the old woman
is quiet as a wilting flower.
The nurse's smile comforts her.
This old woman has not,
out of anger,
turned away from people
or from God.
Like her, my mother
was faithful to heaven
while in the valley of the shadow of death.
But my mother was filled with dread.

ג. אתה טועה

אַתָּה טוֹעֶה
גַּם עַל עֶרֶשׂ דְּוָי
לֹא נָמוֹג הָעַרְפֶּל
גַּם כַּאֲשֶׁר נִגַּשׁ אֵלַי הַמָּוֶת
קָרוֹב עַד אֵימָה
הָיִיתִי רְחוֹקָה תַּ"ק פַּרְסָה עַל תַּ"ק פַּרְסָה
מִן הַחִידָה.

3. You are mistaken

You are mistaken—
even in death's cradle
the fog did not dissolve.
Even when the end was near,
terrifyingly near,
I was miles and miles away
from the riddle.

ד. נפשי הציצה מן החרכים

לרותי פרוידיגר

נַפְשִׁי הֵצִיצָה מִן הַחֲרַכִּים
אֲשֶׁר בְּתוֹךְ הַבּוּקָה וְהַמְּבֻלָּקָה
שֶׁל חַלְיִי.
מִשְׁבְּיָהּ קָרְאָה
לְ־הָיָה הֹוֶה וְיִהְיֶה,
בַּחֹשֶׁךְ לָחֲשָׁה
בְּיָדְךָ אַפְקִיד אֶת רוּחִי, אֶת כְּאֵבִי,
אֶת כְּבוֹדִי, אֶת חַיַּי, וְאֶת מוֹתִי.

4. *My soul peered through the lattices*

For Ruti Freudiger

My soul peered through the lattices
within the desolation and devastation
of my illness.
From its captivity, it called
to Was-Is-Will Be.
In the dark, it whispered,
"In Your hands, I place
my spirit, my pain,
my honor, my life, my death."

ה. כאשר שמעה

כַּאֲשֶׁר שָׁמְעָה הָאִשָּׁה
שְׁחוּמַת הַפָּנִים
שֶׁמֵּרְקָה אֶת הָרִצְפָּה אָז –
אֶת דִּבְרֵי הָרוֹפֵא,
אָמְרָה לִי:
אֲנִי אֶתְפַּלֵּל עָלַיִךְ.
יְדִידָה פִּתְאֹמִית תְּמוֹל לֹא נוֹדַעַת
אָמְרָה לִי:
אֲנִי אֶתְפַּלֵּל עָלַיִךְ.

5. When the woman

When the brown-faced woman—
who was, at that moment,
polishing the floor—
heard the doctor's words,
she said to me,
"I will pray for you."
A sudden, new friend
said to me,
"I will pray for you."

Notes to the Poems

Zelda's poetry is rich with phrases and images borrowed or adapted from Jewish sacred literature. Her many citations and allusions have their sources in Bible, Talmud (rabbinic compilations of law, legends, ethics, and theology, from the third to the fifth centuries), Midrash (homiletic or legal interpretation of the Bible), medieval Jewish philosophy, liturgy, Kabbalah (the mystical tradition that crystallized in Provence and Spain in the eleventh and twelfth centuries), and Hasidic teachings (texts from the eighteenth-century Eastern European mystical revivalist movement). The following notes point out salient references to these sources, and to Jewish practices and traditions with which the general reader may not be familiar. Where the poems touch upon large conceptual categories, I have occasionally appended suggestions for further reading for the interested nonscholar. I have also included a few comments about matters of translation, in cases where the Hebrew is especially ambiguous or where the English versions may seem to diverge in an unlikely way from the originals.

The Old House *(pp. 26–29)*
The steep mountains; *heharim hanishpim* — The meaning of the adjective is uncertain. See Isaiah 13:2: "high (or steep) mountain" (*har nishpeh*). See also Jeremiah 13:16: "mountains of darkness" (*harey nashef*).

Nothingness; *ha'ayin* — The word *ayin*, "nothing" or "nothingness" (*ha'ayin*, "the nothingness"), which recurs multiple times in Zelda's poetry, is deployed as a technical term in Kabbalah, where it denotes the ultimate indescribability of God as beyond all qualities and things. Zelda, who was no doubt familiar with the kabbalistic usage, applied the term in various ways, sometimes associating it, as here, with the abyss, and elsewhere with silence, as in "You Call Out Silence to Me" (p. 109), and even with death, as in "Enchanted Bird" (p. 137). I have capitalized the word in English to indicate its status as a theological term, translating it variously with and without the definite article.

With My Grandfather *(pp. 32–33)*

Like our father Abraham / who counted stars at night; *k'avraham avinu / shebalaylah safar mazalot* — An allusion to God's covenant with Abraham to make his progeny as numerous as the stars. See Genesis 15:5: "And He brought him outside and said, 'Look toward heaven, and count the stars, if you are able to count them.' And He said to him, 'So shall your seed be.'"

Who called out to his Creator / from the furnace; *shekar'a el bor'o / mitokh hakivshan* — B. Talmud, Pesahim 118a, tells a story conveying the piety of Abraham even as he is being thrown into a fiery furnace by King Nimrod. Nimrod seeks to kill Abraham as punishment for his refusal to denounce his God and pay homage to the king; Abraham refuses to capitulate to the king and instead calls upon God, who rescues him. Midrash Genesis Rabbah 38:13 recounts a similar tale about Abraham being thrown into the fiery furnace by Nimrod as punishment for disrespecting his father's idols; here too, Abraham is saved in the end by God.

Who bound his son / on the altar; *she'et b'no akad* — See Genesis 22:1–19, the story of the binding of Isaac.

Perfect faith; *emunah sh'lemah* — The words "I believe with perfect faith" (*ani ma'amin be'emunah sh'lemah*) begin each statement in the "Thirteen Principles," a classic formulation of Jewish creed by the philosopher-theologian Moses Maimonides (1135–1204).

There is no justice, / no judge; *en din v'en dayan* — From an Aramaic phrase in Midrash Leviticus Rabbah 28:1, referring to a state of general lawlessness.

The Heavenly Jerusalem; *y'rushalayim shel ma'lah* — Literally, "Jerusalem of above," a term originating in B. Talmud, Ta'anit 5a. The rabbinic belief was that Jerusalem was built in two parallel parts, the physical Jerusalem "of below" and the spiritual Jerusalem "of above." For more information about this topic, see under "Jerusalem" in the *Encyclopedia Judaica*, vol. 9, 1556–60 ("In the Aggadah") and 1563–64 ("In Kabbalah").

The Crippled Beggar 1 *(pp. 38–41)*
That which is revealed / and that which is hidden; *et hanigla'ot v'et hanistarot* — Deuteronomy 29:28: "That which is hidden belongs to the Lord our God and that which is revealed belongs to us and to our children."

The Carmel in my soul; *hakarmel sheb'nafshi* — Zelda lived for a number of years on Mount Carmel (site of the city of Haifa, on the northwest coast of Israel), and references to it appear in many of her poems. See especially "The Invisible Carmel" (p. 81), which is the title poem of her second book.

The Crippled Beggar 2 *(pp. 42–45)*
A broken reed; *kaneh ratzutz* — See Isaiah 36:6; II Kings 18:21: "That broken reed of a staff," i.e., that which cannot be relied upon; see also Isaiah 42:3.

The Bad Neighbor *(pp. 46–53)*
". . . *and not into temptation, and not into disgrace . . .*"; *"v'lo lidey nisayon v'lo lidey vizayon"* — "Bring us not into the hands of sin . . . and not into the hands of temptation and not into the hands of disgrace," from the morning prayer service.

A crown of royalty; *keter mal'khut* — This phrase serves as the title of a long poem by the Hebrew poet Solomon ibn Gabirol (1021–58), which is sometimes recited after the evening service of Yom Kippur as a private devotion.

"Save me today and every day / from the insolent and from insolence, / from a bad person, and from a bad companion, / and from a bad neighbor"; *"shetatzileni hayom uv'khol yom / me'azey panim ume'azut panim, /me'adam ra, umeḥaver ra / umishakhen ra"* — From a prayer by Rabbi Judah the Prince, in the morning prayer service.

Only when the black waters crashed over my soul; *rak ka'asher av'ru al nafshi / hamayim hash'ḥorim* — See Psalm 124:5: "Then the evil waters would have swept over our soul."

"You, standing there, across the way"; *"at ha'omedet sham mineged"* — The phrase *omedet mineged*, "standing across," may suggest either standing as an opponent or standing aloof. See II Kings 2:7; Obadiah v. 11.

The light of the seven days; *or / shiv'at hayamim* — Isaiah 30:26: "The light of the moon shall be like the light of the sun, and the light of the sun shall be sevenfold, like the light of the seven days."

"Don't imagine"; *"al t'damu b'nafsh'khem"* — A biblical expression, literally, "do not think in (or with) your soul." See, for example, Esther 4:13: "Do not think in your soul that you will escape from the king's house."

On the lyre and the harp; *aley asor va'aley navel* — Psalm 92:4. The specific identifications of these stringed instruments, which appear multiple times in the Bible, are not known. See also Psalm 150:3–4, where the drum (*tof*) and the ram's horn (*shofar*) are mentioned along with the harp (*navel*).

My heart filled; *mal'u k'salay* — Literally, "my innards (or loins) filled." A metaphorical expression, used in biblical Hebrew and in later poetic texts, the closest English equivalent of which is "my heart filled." See Psalm 38:8: "For my loins are filled with burning" (*ki-kh'salay mal'u nikleh*).

252

Moon Is Teaching Bible *(pp. 56–57)*
The Hebrew *kalanit*, anemone, is rendered here as "Poppy," for the
sake of the sound in the English version. The translator begs the
reader's indulgence and offers by way of justification the facts that
the anemone and the poppy are strikingly similar in appearance and
(like the cyclamen, which is also mentioned in the poem) are each
found in the Israeli countryside during early spring.

The personification of nature in this fable-like poem is emphasized
in the Hebrew by the omission of the definite article before some
of the nouns. To highlight this in the English version, I have capi-
talized the names of the nature images—Moon, Cyclamen, Poppy,
Mountain, and Wind.

In the Dry Riverbed *(pp. 58–59)*
Dry riverbed; *nahal akhzav* — Literally, "a deceitful stream," the
term for a creek that flows in winter and dries up in summer (also
known today as a *wadi*). In Jeremiah 15:18, *nahal akhzav* is a meta-
phor for infidelity: "Will you be to me like a deceitful stream, un-
faithful waters?"

Heat wave; *sharav* — The term, which appears in Isaiah 35:7 and
49:10, refers to an oppressively hot weather condition occurring in
Mediterranean countries and brought about by dry desert winds
(also referred to in modern Hebrew as a *hamsin*).

Cain's eye; *eyno shel kayin* — Cain is referred to in rabbinic litera-
ture as "an evil-eyed man" (*ish ra ayin*); see, for example, Midrash
Exodus Rabbah 31:17.

My Peace *(pp. 62–63)*
My peace; *sh'lomi* — The Hebrew can also mean "my well-being," as
in the common greeting *mah sh'lomkha?* ("How are you?"), literally,
"what is your well-being?"

In the last incarnation; *bagilgul hakodem* — The word *gilgul* (here
translated as "incarnation"), whose root means "turn" or "roll," re-
fers to the doctrine of transmigration of souls, that is, the "rolling"

of the soul into another body in a subsequent life. The theory of *gilgul* became one of the major doctrines of Kabbalah, beginning with its first literary expression in *Sefer habahir* in the late twelfth century. For more information, see the article by Gershom Scholem under "Gilgul" in the *Encyclopedia Judaica*, vol. 7, 573–77.

Each Rose *(pp. 66–67)*
"They shall beat their swords . . ."; *"v'khit'tu"* — Isaiah 2:4: "And they shall beat their swords into ploughshares, and their spears into pruning hooks; nation shall not lift up sword against nation, and they shall no longer learn war."

Take a boat / and cross the sea of fire; *kah sirah / vahatzeh et yam ha'esh* — In Merkavah mysticism (see note to "From the Songs of Childhood," this page, below), "the sea of fire" *(yam shel esh)* surrounds the divine throne. See *Seder rabah divreshit*, section 46, which can be found in A. J. Wertheimer, *Batey midrashot* (Jerusalem: 1968), 3–49.

I Stood in Jerusalem *(pp. 68–69)*
Jerusalem . . . smiling like a bride; *y'rushalayim . . . ham'hayekhet k'mo kalah* — Jerusalem is portrayed as a bride in Isaiah 62:5.

I Banished from My Heart *(pp. 72–73)*
For the day had passed; *ki fanah yom* — From a prayer in the concluding service of Yom Kippur (the Day of Atonement), which begins: "Open to us the gates, even as the gates are being locked, for the day has passed." The reference is to the metaphorical gates of life, through which the Jew seeks to pass before the end of the day of prayer.

From the Songs of Childhood *(pp. 76–77)*
A chariot to God; *merkavah le'elohim* — An allusion to *ma'aseh merkavah*, Merkavah ("chariot") mysticism, a school of interpretation that takes its symbols from Ezekiel's vision of a divine throne being transported through heaven (Ezekiel, chap. 1). The texts of Merkavah mysticism were composed mostly between the third and sixth centuries in Babylonia; the themes were developed further

in Kabbalah (beginning in the twelfth century) and, still later, in Hasidism. For more information, see the article by Gershom Scholem under "Merkabah Mysticism" in the *Encyclopedia Judaica*, vol. 11, 1386–90.

The poem also calls to mind two classical myths, which may or may not have been intentional allusions on the part of the poet. The first is about the artificer Daedalus, who fashioned a pair of wings for his son Icarus, cautioning him not to fly too close to the sun. When Icarus ignored his father's warning and flew too high, the sun melted the wings, causing them to fall off and Icarus to plummet to the sea. The second myth tells the story of Phaeton, half-mortal son of Helios (the sun), who tried to drive his father's chariot across the sky but lost control, causing the earth to burn. To keep the earth from being destroyed, Zeus hurled a thunderbolt at Phaeton, striking him dead, shattering the chariot, and plunging the horses into the sea.

Went forth; *halokh hal'khu* — This verbal construction, which opens the biblical parable of Jotham (Judges 9:8–15), lends the poem the tone of a fairy tale.

The Invisible Carmel *(pp. 80–81)*
For information about the Carmel, see the note to "The Crippled Beggar 1" (p. 251).

To the Supreme One; *la'elyon al hakol* — Literally, "the one above all," a phrase deriving from Deuteronomy 26:19: "He will set you above all the nations *(elyon al kol-hagoyim)*" and Deuteronomy 28: 1: "The Lord your God will set you above all the nations of the earth *(elyon al kol-goyey ha'aretz)*." The term *el elyon*, literally, "supreme God," is found multiple times in the Bible; Zelda creates a similar appellation with *elyon al kol*.

[In his eyes, birds of paradise] *(pp. 82–83)*
In his eyes, birds of paradise / were singing / and gold feathers drifted / onto the books; *b'eynav hayu sharot / tziporey gan eden / v'notzot shel zahav nash'ru / al has'farim* — The bird of paradise

(*tzipor eden*) is a member of the family of songbirds *Paradiseidae*, native to the New Guinea region. The male of the species is noted for its long tail feathers and the metallic sheen of its brilliantly colored plumage.

A pious man; *ba'al halakhah* — Literally, "master of Jewish law," a term found in late Jewish legalistic literature.

New Fruit in the Season of Childhood (*pp. 84–99*)
The text of the Hebrew poem as it appears in the edition of Zelda's collected poems, *Shirey Zelda*, differs from that found in the original volume in which the poem appeared, *Hakarmel ha'i-nir'eh* (The Invisible Carmel), in that lines 117–20 have a different internal order. The text of the original volume is the more coherent and has been presented here; the translation follows accordingly.

"*What is man that You should remember him?*"; "*mah enosh ki tizk'renu*" — Psalm 8:5, a verse traditionally recited at memorial services.

Because his soul yearned; *ki kaltah nafsho* — See Psalms 84:3; 119: 81.

When I tore my thin dress / to mark my childhood / with a sign of mourning; *ka'asher karati simlati hadakah / l'samen b'ot evel et yalduti* — In Judaism, it is traditional to tear one's clothing after the death of a close relative and to wear the torn clothing throughout the initial stage of the mourning period.

The song of the grasses; *nigun ha'asavim* — A reference to a well-known prayer by the Hasidic master Rabbi Nahman of Bratslav (1770–1811), in which every blade of grass, like every shepherd, is said to have its own unique melody, out of which the prayers of the heart are made.

Whose entrance the cherubs do not guard / with the fiery, ever-turning sword; *shek'ruvim enam shom'rim l'fit'ho / b'lahat haherev hamithapekhet* — In the story of Adam and Eve's banishment from Eden, God stations cherubs and a "fiery, ever-turning sword" to guard the way to the tree of life (Genesis 3:24).

"You enticed me, God, / and I was enticed"; *"pititani adonay va'efat"* — Jeremiah 20:7.

"In God I trust, / I am not afraid, / what can mortals do to me?"; *"be'lohim batahti lo ira mah-ya'aseh vasar li"* — Psalm 56:5.

Silver-everlasting; *almavet hakesef* — *Paronychia argentea*, a white wildflower commonly found in the coastal plain and mountains of Israel, as well as in other Mediterranean countries.

Hidden in the house; *has'funah babayit* — See Hagai 1:4.

The Sun Lit a Wet Branch *(pp. 100–101)*
Distant signs / . . . ancient wonders; *otot r'hokim* / . . . *moftim atikim* — "Signs and wonders" (*otot umoftim*) is a biblical fixed pair (two words commonly linked together) referring to God's miracles. It recurs multiple times: Deuteronomy 4:34; 6:22; 7:19; 26:8; 29:2; 34:11; Isaiah 8:18; Jeremiah 32:20, 21; Psalm 135:9; and Nehemiah 9:10.

For the Light Is My Joy *(pp. 102–5)*
The references to Jonah in the last two stanzas are to the biblical prophet who goes to sea to flee God's command to prophesy. When the sea becomes stormy, Jonah is held accountable by his shipmates and reluctantly thrown overboard, where he is swallowed by a great fish. From the belly of the fish, Jonah begs God's mercy. At the end of the tale, Jonah rests on dry land beneath the shade of a gourd tree provided by God. When the tree withers and dies, Jonah despairs and asks God to let him die, too. N.B.: The word *tzel*, translated in line 21 of the English as "shadow," also means "shade" (Jonah 4:5–6).

Be Not Far *(pp. 106–7)*
Be not far; *al tirhak* — This phrase, which appears as both the title and line 12 of the Hebrew, also serves as the title of Zelda's third book. It is borrowed from the Bible, where it occurs five times (Psalms 22:12; 20; 35:22; 38:22; and 71:12), in each instance addressed, as here, to God.

The valley of the shadow of death; *gey tzalmavet* — Psalm 23:4.

Aimed at you; *negd'kha* — Literally, "across from you" or "against you"; the meaning of the Hebrew is ambiguous.

Let not millions of light-years / stand as a barrier / between You and Job; *al ya'amdu k'hayitz / milyoney sh'not or / ben'kha uven iyov* — See the biblical book of Job, which recounts the story of a man tested by God with great losses and suffering.

You Call Out Silence to Me *(pp. 108–9)*
Nothingness; *ha'ayin* — See the note to "The Old House" (p. 249).

I will not distinguish / living water from empty wells; *lo avhin / ben mayim hayim / l'vorot nishbarim* — Literally, "I will not distinguish living water from broken cisterns." See Jeremiah 2:13: "For My people has committed two evils: they have forsaken Me, the fountain of living water, and hewed themselves cisterns, broken cisterns, that can hold no water."

[I lie in my house] *(pp. 112–13)*
Wanders through the dark; *bahoshekh yahalokh* — Literally, "walks (or goes) in the dark." See Isaiah 9:1: "The people that walked in the dark have seen a great light."

Black Rose *(pp. 118–19)*
In the land of the living; *b'eretz hahayim* — Psalm 116:9: "I will walk before God in the lands of the living."

When I Said the Blessing over the Candles *(pp. 120–21)*
The lands of the living; *artzot hahayim* — See above.

258

My roots are above; *shorashay l'ma'lah* — See II Kings 19:30; Isaiah 37:31: "The remnant that escaped of the house of Judah shall take root downward and bear fruit upward." The natural order—roots below and fruit above—which appears as an image of salvation in these biblical passages, is reversed in Zelda's poem, conveying the speaker's anguish. "Roots above" also suggests the kabbalistic portrayal of the ten emanations (*s'firot*) of the godhead as an inverted tree whose roots lie in the upper realms and whose branches extend through the cosmos.

My soul will depart; *tetze nishmati* — An idiom for dying; see B. Talmud, Ta'anit 21a.

When the King Was Alive (*pp. 122–23*)
The glory of the princess / was within; *hayah k'vod bat hamelekh / p'nimah* — A variation on a difficult phrase in Psalm 45:14, literally, "all the honor of the king's daughter is inside" (*kol-k'vudah vat melekh p'nimah*), which, within Orthodox Judaism, is understood as referring to the modesty in dress and behavior that is required of women.

Cast Me Not Away (*pp. 124–27*)
Ever-dwelling; *shokhen ad* — A phrase from Isaiah 57:15, used in the Sabbath morning service as an appellation for God. In Zelda's poem, it is ambiguous whether the phrase is an appositive indicating direct address of God or an adjective describing the speaker's cry.

Cast me not away from Your presence; al tashlikheni mil'fanekha — Psalm 51:13.

Do not hide Your face from me; al tastir panekha mimeni — See Psalm 13:2.

The Fine Sand, the Terrible Sand (*pp. 128–31*)
If my soul lies down on its side; *im nafshi al tzidah tishkav* — See Ezekiel 4:4.

Let Your Voice Be Heard, O Morning Blessings *(pp. 132–35)*
Morning blessings; blessings of the dawn; *birkhot hashaḥar* — The opening section of the morning prayer service.

Soul mate; *y'did nefesh* — Literally, "friend of the soul." *Y'did nefesh* is the name of a liturgical poem about union with God, composed by the sixteenth-century kabbalist Rabbi Eleazar ben Moses Azikri.

Angel of redemption; *hamal'akh hago'el* — See Genesis 48:16.

Comfort ye, comfort ye; *naḥamu naḥamu* — The opening words of Isaiah 40:1, the first of seven prophetic readings of consolation recited on the seven Sabbaths between Tish'ah B'Av (a day of mourning) and Rosh Hashanah (the New Year).

Enchanted Bird *(pp. 136–37)*
For out of the scent of Nothingness / the tree blossoms — ; *mere'ah ha'ayin yafri'aḥ* — See Job 14:9: "From the scent of water it will blossom" (*mere'ah mayim yafri'aḥ*).

Concerning "Nothingness" (*ha'ayin*), see the note to "The Old House" (p. 249).

Glorious, beautiful; *hadur na'eh* — A phrase from the liturgical poem *Y'did nefesh* (see note to "Let Your Voice Be Heard, O Morning Blessings," above).

Each of Us Has a Name *(pp. 140–43)*
Each of us has a name; *l'khol ish yesh shem* — Literally, "every man (or person) has a name." Because all Hebrew nouns have gender, there is no gender-neutral term in Hebrew for "person"; the word *ish* serves as both "person" and "man." On the assumption that Zelda meant to refer equally to women, I avoided the repeated use of the English masculine pronoun and instead employed the (gender-neutral) first-person plural throughout the poem, e.g., "Each of us has a name . . . given by our parents" instead of "Each person has a name . . . given by his parents."

The poem is an elaboration on a rabbinic theme. See Midrash Eccle-siastes Rabbah 7:1: "A person is called by three names: one that his father and mother call him by, one that others call him by, and one that he is called in the book telling the story of his creation"; see also Midrash Tanhuma, Parashat Vayak'hel: "One finds three names by which a person is called: one that his father and mother call him by, one that people call him by, and one that he acquires for himself. The best of all is that which he acquires for himself."

All Night I Wept *(pp. 144–45)*
All night I implored; *kol halaylah hipalti tahanunay* — See Daniel 9:18.

Though I am dust; *afilu ani afar* — Genesis 18:27.

Before entering the sleep of death; *b'terem ishan hamavet* — See Psalm 13:4.

Place of Fire *(pp. 146–49)*
City / upon whose neck / a loving prophet hung / sapphires, tur-quoise, and rubies; *ir / shenavi ohev / talah al tzavarah / sapirim nofekh v'khadkod* — Sapphires and rubies are found in Isaiah 54: 11–12, a prophecy of consolation for Jerusalem. Sapphires and tur-quoise are two of the gems in the priestly breastplate; see Exodus 28:18.

[I do not like all trees equally] *(pp. 152–55)*
King David's violated daughter; *bito ham'unah shel david hamelekh* — The reference is to Tamar, who was raped and then scorned by her half brother Amnon; see II Samuel 13:1–22 .

The crown of its freshness has fallen; *naf'lah ateret ra'ananuto* — See Lamentations 5:16: "The crown of our head has fallen" (*naf'lah ateret roshenu*), an image of devastation and disgrace.

On the day of God's wrath; *b'yom af adonay* — Zephaniah 2:2–3; Lamentations 2:22.

Yom Kippur Eve *(pp. 156–57)*
Yom Kippur, the Day of Atonement, is the most sacred day of the Jewish year. It marks the end of the season of Rosh Hashanah, the Jewish New Year festival, which is also known as "the birthday of the world." Hence, "from experiences ended / to experiences begun" and "the beginning of time."

[The shadow of the white mountain] *(pp. 160–63)*
The joy / of a bride and groom; *m'sos hatan v'khalah* — Isaiah 62:5.

Creator of man; *yotzer ha'adam* — An appellation for God found in the third and fourth of the seven blessings (*sheva b'rakhot*) recited at Jewish wedding ceremonies.

Let their building / be everlasting; *sheyihyeh binyanam / binyan adey-ad* — Binyan adey-ad, "an everlasting building," appears in the fourth of the seven wedding blessings. In rabbinic literature, it has been interpreted as referring to Eve, who was "built" by God from Adam's rib. See Rashi on Genesis 2:22.

I sat in the shade of the gourd tree; *yashavti b'tzel hakikayon* — The prophet Jonah sat in the shade of a gourd tree after having been rescued from the sea (Jonah 4:5–6). See the note to "For the Light Is My Joy," p. 257.

Mephiboshet *(pp. 164–65)*
Mephiboshet, whose name has been traditionally interpreted to mean "from the mouth of shame," was the son of the biblical Jonathan, bosom friend of King David. The following is a synopsis of Mephiboshet's life, as recounted in II Samuel 4:4; 9:1–13; 16:1–4; 19:25–31: At the age of five, Mephiboshet fell and became crippled, after which, out of loyalty to Jonathan, King David took Mephiboshet under his wing and gave him a servant, Ziba. Ziba later deceived Mephiboshet and lied to David, telling him that Mephiboshet was trying to usurp the throne; because of this, David seized Mephiboshet's property and gave it to Ziba. When ultimately the truth was revealed, David, who was indebted to Ziba for his aid in battle, divided Mephiboshet's estate between the two men.

Mephiboshet then declared that he would not mind relinquishing his entire estate to his betrayor, so grateful was he that David had survived the battle.

Void-and-chaos; *tohu vavohu* — The primordial matter of the creation story; see Genesis 1:2.

The ancient serpent; *hanaḥash hakadmoni* — Rabbinic term for the snake that tricked Adam and Eve in the garden of Eden; see B. Talmud, Sanhedrin 29a. In Kabbalah, the primordial serpent appears frequently, symbolizing the demonic; see, for example, the Zohar 1:12b.

Distant Shame *(pp. 166–69)*
See the note to "Mephiboshet" (p. 262).

[I awoke — the house was lit] *(pp. 172–73)*
I awoke— the house was lit; *va'ikatz v'hiney habayit mu'ar* — The opening two words of the Hebrew, *va'ikatz v'hiney*, literally, "I awoke, and behold," are characteristic of biblical tales of dreams. See Genesis 41:7: "Pharaoh awoke, and, behold, it was a dream" and I Kings 3:15: "Solomon awoke, and, behold, it was a dream."

But no one was there with me; *akh en ish iti babayit* — Literally, "but no man (or person) was there with me in the house." As explained above (see note to "Each of Us Has a Name," p. 260), *ish* means both "person" and "man"; hence, the line could be alternatively translated "but no man was there with me." See Genesis 39: 11, the story of Potiphar's wife: "There was no man from the men of the house there in the house" (*v'en ish me'anshey habayit sham babayit*).

And surely a mountain, / and surely fire; *vahalo har / vahalo esh* — The mountain and fire call to mind the description of the giving of Torah at Mount Sinai (Exodus 19:16–18), to which the poet refers more directly in other poems (see, for example, "[I shall not float unreined]," p. 231). *Halo har halo esh* (Surely a Mountain, Surely Fire) is the title of Zelda's fourth book.

In My Dream *(pp. 180–81)*
As a tree planted beside streams of water; *k'etz shatul al palgey mayim* — Psalm 1:3; see also Jeremiah 17:8.

The Friendship of the White Jasmine *(pp. 182–83)*
My soul dozes off, / dreaming of a fountain; *m'namnemet nafshi / holemet al ma'yan* — In the allegorical tale "The Seven Beggars" by the Hasidic master Rabbi Nahman of Bratslav, the love between the heart of the world and a fountain expresses the yearning of humanity for union with God, which will bring about the unification of the world.

Jasmine Branch *(pp. 184–85)*
And did not return to dust; *v'lo shav l'afar* — Genesis 3:19: "For you are dust, and to dust you shall return"; Job 34:15: "And man shall return to dust."

The Fine Light of My Peace *(pp. 188–89)*
Heavenly letters; *otiyot shel ma'lah* — Literally, "letters (or signs) of above." In Kabbalah, these are the supernal letters, ideal forms of the letters of the alphabet through which God is believed to have created the universe; see *Sefer y'tzirah* 2:1–5.

[The first rain—] *(pp. 192–93)*
With no sign of Cain; *b'li ot shel kayin* — See Genesis 4:15: "And God put a sign on Cain" (to protect him from being killed, after exiling him for the murder of his brother, Abel).

A plenitude of freshness; *alfey r'vavah ra'ananut* — *Alfey r'vavah*, literally, "thousands of myriads," is a biblical expression meaning "multitudes." See Genesis 24:60.

The abyss conjures up; *hat'hom ma'aleh* — See Ezekiel 26:19: "When I raise upon you the abyss" (*b'ha'alot alayikh et-t'hom*). Zelda inverts the biblical image, making the abyss the subject of the phrase rather than the object of the verb.

The Tree of Life *(pp. 202–3)*
The tree of life; *etz hahayim* — See Genesis 2:9; 3:22; and 3:24 (the story of the garden of Eden). Zelda's use of *etz hahayim* as a metaphor is in keeping with several usages of the indefinite form of the term (*etz hayim*, "tree of life") in Proverbs 3:18; 11:30; 13:12; and 15:4.

Full of wisdom; *uvsom sekhel* — Literally, "and giving sense." See Nehemiah 8:8. In the collected edition of Zelda's Hebrew poems, *Shirey Zelda*, this phrase has been vocalized differently, to read *uvshum sekhel*, "and without sense." Vocalizations are typically not inserted by authors but are added during the editing process; hence, they are not always accurate representations of the author's intended meaning. *Uvshum sekhel* is incongruous in context, and is, additionally, in a lower diction than the rest of the poem; *uvsom sekhel* is not only compatible with the meaning of the poem but, as a biblical idiom, is in keeping with the poem's tone. For these reasons, the vocalization in this volume departs from that of the earlier Hebrew editions; the translation follows accordingly.

[There was something startling] *(pp. 204–5)*
That His mercy had not ceased; *ki lo kalu rahamav* — Lamentations 3:22.

Uncombed Hair *(pp. 208–11)*
Hagar was the handmaiden of Sarai (later renamed Sarah), wife of the biblical patriarch Abram (later, Abraham). In Genesis, Hagar is visited twice by an angel in the wilderness. The first incident (Genesis 16) occurs after Hagar goes to the desert to flee her mistress; an angel appears to her beside a spring and tells her to return home because she is to bear Abram's son. Later, after Hagar's son Ishmael is born, both mother and son are cast out by Sarah into the wilderness, where Hagar fears for Ishmael's life. In this story (Genesis 21:9–21), an angel appears and shows Hagar a well, from which she gives Ishmael water to drink.

Island *(pp. 212–13)*
Like those who jumped ship / to stand on the back of a whale; *k'otam p'litey oniyah / she'am'du al gabo shel livyatan* — This image derives from a talmudic story attributed to Rabbah bar Bar Hanah: "Once, while traveling on a ship, we saw a fish whose back was covered with sand, out of which grass was growing. Thinking that we had come upon dry land, we went up and baked and cooked on the fish's back. When the fish's back became hot, the fish turned over, and had the ship not been nearby, we would have drowned." See B. Talmud, Bava Batra 73a–b.

In the Moon's Domain *(pp. 214–15)*
Dust and ashes; *afar va'efer* — A biblical expression referring to the lowliness and impermanence of human beings in relation to God. See Genesis 18:27; Job: 30:19; 42:6.

Heavy Silence *(pp. 220–21)*
The names that humans have given / to the birds of the sky / and the beasts of the field; *hashemot / shenatan ha'adam l'ofot hashamayim / ulhayot hasadeh* — See the naming of the animals in the creation story, Genesis 2:19–20.

And things hidden from the eye; *v'lidvarim s'muyim min ha'ayin* — See B. Talmud, Ta'anit 8b: "The blessing is to be found nowhere . . . but in something hidden from the eye."

Knower of Mysteries; *yode'a ta'alumot* — Psalm 43:22: "For He knows the mysteries of the heart" (*ki-hu yode'a ta'alumot lev*).

On That Night of Stars *(pp. 224–25)*
Years that spill like water; *hashanim shenigarot kamayim* — See II Samuel 14:4: *mayim nigarim*, "water that is poured out (or spilled)" and Micah 1:4: *mayim mugarim*, "water that overflows (or cascades)."

Distances / beyond all distance; *merhakim / shenivd'lu mikol merhak* — Literally, "distances that are separated (or distinct) from all distance." The phrase *shenivd'lu mikol merḥak* serves as the title of Zelda's sixth collection.

Pause *(pp. 226–29)*
When a river flowed from his inner Eden; *ka'asher yatza nahar me'eden p'nimiyuto* — See Genesis 2:10.

Wells rich with water; *ma'yanot nikhb'dey mayim* — Proverbs 8:24.

[I shall not float unreined] *(pp. 230–31)*
The lightning and thunder / that I heard at Sinai; *hab'rakim v'hakolot / sheshamati b'sinay* — The reference is to the giving of Torah at Mount Sinai; see Exodus 19:16–18. Traditional belief holds that every Jewish soul, past and present, stood at Sinai and heard the word of God.

When Yearnings *(pp. 232–33)*
You have burdened me; *hayitem alay la'torah* — See Isaiah 1:14.

In the Hospital: Beyond the wall, a sick old woman *(pp. 240–41)*
The valley of the shadow of death; *gey tzalmavet* — Psalm 23:4.

In the Hospital: You are mistaken *(pp. 242–43)*
Miles and miles; *tak parsah al tak parsah* — Literally, "five hundred parasangs," a rabbinic expression for great distances. See B. Talmud, Bava Kama 82b.

In the Hospital: My soul peered through the lattices *(pp. 244–45)*
Peered through the lattices; *hetzitzah min haḥarakim* — See Song of Songs 2:9; the reference is to the lover peering through the lattices of his beloved's house.

The desolation and devastation; *habukah v'ham'vulakah* — The phrase is adapted from a three-word biblical phrase, *bukah um'vukah um'vulakah*, "desolation (or emptiness) and devastation and ruin" (Nahum 2:11). The original context is a prophecy of God's destruction of the city of Nineveh. The juxtaposition of this phrase with the above phrases from the Song of Songs is stark, even jarring, in its emotional contrast.

To Was-Is-Will Be; *l-hayah hoveh v'yihyeh* — This appellation for God, as well as the phrase cited below, appear in the liturgical hymn *Adon olam*, "Lord of the World," attributed to the eleventh-century Hebrew poet Solomon ibn Gabirol, although possibly authored much earlier. The themes of the hymn, which is used in Jewish prayer services worldwide, are the eternity and unity of God, along with human trust in God's providence.

In Your hands, I place / my spirit; *b'yad'kha afkid et ruhi* — The original source of these words from *Adon olam* is Psalm 31:6.

Acknowledgments

This book was three decades in the making, and during that time a number of people contributed to it invaluably. The poet herself was an inspiration to me throughout the course of our friendship, generously sharing her world over Sabbath meals and afternoon cups of tea. Knowing Zelda enriched both my work and my life.

I am grateful for the gifts of other friends as well—beginning with Snira Klein, whose love of Hebrew poetry is matched by an intuitive grasp of its nuances and beauties. It is always a pleasure reading poems with Snira, and I can only begin to thank her for the many hours we spent together immersed in Zelda's lines.

I benefitted greatly from the wealth of knowledge brought to Zelda's text by Yair Zakovitch, who pointed out biblical references I might otherwise have missed. Daniel Matt and Avigdor Shinan helped me identify obscure rabbinic and kabbalistic sources. Ezri Uval, of blessed memory, lent a Hebraist's eye to an early draft of the translations, reviewing them for accuracy. Lucy Day and Lynne Knight read the English versions for poetic style and offered suggestions for the Introduction. I enjoyed conversations with Ron Kuzar about Zelda's language and with Rochelle Furstenberg about Zelda's life. My gratitude to all who shared their expertise with me.

Special thanks to Izzy Pludwinski, creator of the beautiful Hebrew typeface that appears on the cover and title page, for his help with the cover design. Thanks, too, to painters Nancy Andell, Julian Cooper, and Karen O'Neil for consultation on the cover art.

My deep appreciation to Barbara Selya, the indefatigable managing editor of Hebrew Union College Press, for graciously ushering the book through every stage of its production. A dedicated editor is a gift beyond measure.

Two subsidized residencies at the MacDowell Colony gave me undistracted time for writing. In its final stage, this project was awarded a grant from the Hadassah-Brandeis Institute. I am grateful to these institutions for providing me with what writers often need most—the time and means to get the work done.

Above all, I am indebted to Steve Rood, poet and critic par excellence, who viewed draft after draft of the manuscript, never seeming to tire of any of it. When I found myself struggling with what seemed like the hundredth version of a poem, still not satisfied, Steve's finely honed observations gave me fresh appreciation for both the text and the task.

Marcia Falk
Berkeley, California
2004 / 5764

Marcia Falk's poems, translations, and essays have been published widely in literary magazines and anthologies. She is the author of a groundbreaking new Hebrew and English prayer book written from a nonhierarchical, gender-inclusive perspective, *The Book of Blessings: New Jewish Prayers for Daily Life, the Sabbath, and the New Moon Festival* (HarperCollins; paperback, Beacon Press). Her other books include an acclaimed translation of *The Song of Songs* (University Press of New England / Brandeis University Press); an annotated volume of translations from the Yiddish of the twentieth-century poet Malka Heifetz Tussman, *With Teeth in the Earth* (Wayne State University Press); and two chapbooks of poems, *This Year in Jerusalem* (State Street Press) and *It Is July in Virginia* (Rara Avis Press), which won the Gertrude Claytor Award of the Poetry Society of America.

She received a B.A. in philosophy from Brandeis University and a Ph.D. in English and comparative literature from Stanford; she was a Fulbright Scholar and later a Postdoctoral Fellow in Hebrew literature and Bible at the Hebrew University of Jerusalem. She has been a professor of English, creative writing, Hebrew literature, and Judaic studies at SUNY Binghamton, the Claremont Colleges, and Stanford, and she held the Sally Priesand Chair in Jewish Women's Studies at Hebrew Union College in Cincinnati.

A life member of the Art Students League in New York, Marcia Falk trained as a painter in her youth and recently returned to painting; one of her oil pastels appears on the cover of this book. She is now at work on a series of paintings to accompany literary texts. She also continues to teach poetry classes and workshops and to lecture widely on Jewish feminism, Jewish women's literature, and other topics. Her artwork and descriptions of her programs may be seen at www.marciafalk.com.

About the Typefaces

The English text of *The Spectacular Difference* is set in Transitional 521, created by the modern American artist, book designer, and calligrapher W. A. Dwiggins. It is based on his famous 1935 Linotype typeface Electra.

The English display fonts are Diotima and Diotima Italic, the former designed in 1948 and the latter in 1929 by the German typographer Gudrun Zapf von Hesse. Diotima is named for the priestess in Plato's *Symposium* who teaches Socrates about love.

The Hebrew poems are set in David and David Light, part of a family of fonts created in 1952 by the German Jewish artist and calligrapher Ismar David. An elegant typeface with a clean, modern look, David is widely considered to be a classic in Hebrew typography.

The Hebrew display face is Shir, an innovative font designed in 1998 by the American-born Hebrew scribe and calligrapher Izzy Pludwinski, in Jerusalem. Shir (the name means *poem* or *song*), which was the outgrowth of calligraphic experimentation, is based on Hebrew cursive forms and is particularly suited to lyric texts.